When Doves Cry

STORIES THAT HEAL

COMPILATION BY
NEPHETINA L. SERRANO

When Doves Cry: Stories That Heal

Copyright © 2017 Compiled by Nephetina L. Serrano

Published in the United States of America by

Gospel 4 U Network

All rights reserved. No part of this book may be reproduced or transmitted in anyway by tmeans, electronic, mechanical, Photocopy, recording or oherwise, without prior permission of the author except as provided by USA copyright law.

Scriptures are taken from the

Holy Bible King James Version
unless otherwise marked.

ISBN - 978-0-9984665-6-9

Library of Congress Number 2017912843

Printed in United States of America

September 2017

Contents

DEDICATION

ACKNOWLEDGEMENT

FOREWORD …………....Dr. Annette V. Hampton

INTRODUCTION ……........Nephetina L. Serrano

Chapter One: Forgetting Those Things

    By: Carla Greene …………………............15

Chapter Two: There Is Joy in Your Mourning

    By: Staci Morgan Boyd ……………...........27

Chapter Three: I Am the Gift She Left Behind

    By: Julia D. Ford ……………....................41

Chapter Four: It's Never Too Late

    By: Roneve Davis …………………….......55

Chapter Five: The Goodness of the Lord

    By: Andrea Riley …………………….....67

Chapter Six: Heaven Bound

    By: Jennifer Marlowe ……………………83

Chapter Seven: If Not For God

    By: Senator LeAnna Washington 99

Chapter Eight: From Crushed ... to Joy!

    By: Dr. Mary Floyd Palmer ……….............113

Chapter Nine: Gone Now but Never Forgotten

    By: Dr. Joanna Birchett ………….............127

Chapter Ten: Though Forsaken…Received by the Lord

    By: Corrie Lingenfelter ………….............141

Chapter Eleven: The Virtuous Mother

    By: Deidra Roussaw …………..................151

Chapter Twelve: Pain of Promise

    By: Emma Jean Brant ………………........167

Special Reflections:

My Mother, a Priceless Treasure

    By: Terry Moragne-Macon ……………......181

One of a Kind Mother

    By: Carolyn Trumpler-Davis …………........191

Dedication

I dedicate this book to all women, young and old, who have lost their mothers. It is my prayer that through this inspirational journal women's lives, in every state and around the world, will be touched. It is my hope they will find comfort, peace, joy, and encouragement to journey on in this life, knowing that God is carrying them through even this ordeal.

> *"Weeping may endure for a night, but joy cometh in the morning."* (Ps. 30:5 KJV)

Acknowledgement

A heartfelt thank you to the co-authors, siblings, family and friends who made this book possible through much prayer, encouragement and patience. God, my Father who gave me the vision and dream and all the tools to birth out this baby. He encouraged me and reassured me He had given me this assignment therefore, I know it will go far and bless many.

To the love of my life, my king and the prince in our home, my husband Richard Serrano, I want you to know I appreciate the support, prayers and nights you went to bed without me. You were my biggest strength throughout this entire process. I love you so very much "forever your queen".

My mom Elder, Emma Jean Brant, who was second to know what God had spoken to me to do and the first to say yes to being a co-author. I love and honor you for showing me how to hold on to God's unchanging hand. You have demonstrated the power of a praying mother. Thank you for always believing in me.

My Bishop Ernest C. Morris, Sr. and Mother Winifred Morris. Bishop you always taught us if God spoke to our heart to do something just do it, don't wait on others, you start it. You are a big inspiration to both me and my husband and it has been a pleasure, joy and privilege to have served you and to be a member of Mt Airy Church of God In Christ for the past 27 yrs. Mother Morris, I never stopped dreaming because of you and many doors opened to me because you were praying for me. I thank you so much, you are my secret hero, well not anymore, now the world knows.

My "Bestie" and friend of more than 30 years Minister, Dr. Bernadette Camp. Through good, bad, happy, sad and sister quarrels you never stop loving and praying for me. You gave me another family to love me and that they do. I am a very proud auntie.

My CLC Book center family of Cedarbrook Plaza, Wyncote, Pennsylvania. You have embraced my husband and I and the work we do with couples by having us do workshops and supporting events. Thank you for believing in the sanctity of Covenant Marriage and the family. More importantly, supporting local ministries in their quest to share the Good News of Christ.

For the many women of God and women in leadership that said yes to this book collaboration, I love and appreciate you. I am forever grateful to God for putting us all together. There is no doubt that you and I are a part of something great. It has been an honor to work with you all. Special thanks to Gospel 4 U Publishing team for pushing us through to the end. God bless you all always!

WHEN DOVES CRY

Foreword

Life has a way of dispensing hard blows to us from time to time. One critical blow can be the death of a loved one. While most understand this as just part of the life cycle, it is nevertheless a hard, difficult, and depressing event to experience. Death is a dreadful tragedy, but when it involves the most beloved person in our lives—like our mothers—then in many ways it is earth shattering. This book, *"When Doves Cry,"* shares stories about this difficult experience. The authors share personal journeys through grief, coping strategies, acceptance of loss, faith that sustained through challenging times, and eventually growing despite this devastating episode.

Mothers, in many ways, are the central persons in

our lives. When a mother passes away, quite often people ask the question, "How am I going to go on without her?" While I know there are exceptions, because there are some mothers who are struggling with personal issues, generally many would admit that their mother played a pivotal role in their lives, and she is often considered the most significant reliable human being on the planet.

In reading the stories shared in this book, it is the hope of its authors that you will be challenged to show empathy during someone else's journey, appreciate the legacy that mothers leave behind, grow to trust the God who called your mother to rest, and learn how to help people who have lost a loved one, rather than hurting them during this vulnerable period in their lives. During this defenseless time, the sovereignty of God may be questioned. Remember how Job, this blameless and upright man, reacted to the loss of his whole family, his possessions and his health as well. This man of faith went through a hard struggle, swinging the whole time between faith and doubt. But in the end, Job found his comfort in the sovereignty of God. The pain and hurt experienced by the loss of a loved one can be overwhelming. This feeling of instability produces insecurity, and makes it feel like your whole world is falling apart. This is not the time to run away from God but to run to God. His name is our one and only refuge (Prov. 18: 10). Even in our loss, God still loves us with an everlasting love. In this book, the strength one gains from a relationship with God is rightly underscored. Read, listen, and learn as you journey through *"When Doves Cry."*

Dr. Annette V. Hampton
Dean At Christian Research
And Development

WHEN DOVES CRY

Introduction

Stories That Heal

"When Doves Cry" was birthed out of a dream and a desire to see women healed from the hurt, pain, and devastating loss of a mother. Our desire is to see women live life victoriously, knowing that God will see them through every moment and stage of grief, so that they would be able to live again.

This twelve-month Inspirational Journal will inspire, uplift, and encourage women of all ages who have lost their mothers to share their difficulties, happy and sad times, moments of disappointments, triumphs, and victories. In this book, you will be taken on a journey, giving you a place to go to while you travel alongside your sisters and share their stories. You will gain strength, courage, wisdom, comfort, and understanding. These women will share the good, the bad, and sometimes the ugly things in their relationships with their mothers, or lack thereof. You will be filled with words of inspiration, encouragement, and hope. You will also be reassured, and inspired, as these ladies take on transparency in sharing words of hope and healing, letting you know that life is still worth living and that you can make it through every trial, disappointment, or horrible situation.

As you journey through the reflections of your sisters, you will discover you are not alone; these women are right there with you to share their joys and sorrows. You will soon realize that JOY does come with the morning (Ps. 30:5). These women are here to journey with you as you begin to Live Again!

What You Can Expect on the Journey

The loss of any loved one is challenging, but especially the loss of a mom. Grief is a process that takes time to heal; it takes you through stages, and one never knows when the pain or devastation will go away. Knowing the 5 stages of grief can help you identify where you are in the process. These stages can help you to be patient with yourself, telling you it's okay to grieve.

I encourage you to take time to see where you are in this process of grief, to begin with denial, anger, bargaining, depression, and acceptance. Don't be afraid to take the journey toward healing. Remember, God is with you through every stage. Do not let these precious words leave your heart: *"Even though I walk through the valley of the shadow of death, I will fear no evil, for you are with me; your rod and your staff, they comfort me"* (Ps. 23:4).

You will read every woman's personal story, moments of reflection, "Speak life," and words of encouragement. Every one of them will share a personal or favorite Scripture of choice, words of comfort and/or exhortation, a declaration, and a personal prayer. Lastly, a short Biography and contact information for each woman will be at the end of this book.

"He [God] will wipe away every tear from their eyes,
and death shall be no more,
neither shall there be mourning, nor crying, nor pain
anymore,
for the former things have passed away." (Rev. 21:4)

It is my sincere prayer that you will be blessed after reading these amazing stories and that you learn to Live Again!

Nephetina L. Serrano

COMPILED BY NEPHETINA L. SERRANO

WHEN DOVES CRY
STORIES THAT HEAL

WHEN DOVES CRY

Chapter One
Forgetting Those Things
By: Carla Greene

Have you ever had a precious piece of jewelry that was elegant and costly, or simple but uniquely crafted? Have you ever misplaced that precious piece, that special item, and forgotten where you misplaced it? Have you searched for it in all those familiar places, in the drawer, in the jewelry box, or on the dresser? Have you thought that you possibly dropped it and began searching for it under the couch, behind the bed, or in the bottom of your purse?

Just like that precious lost piece, I've struggled for years with the lost memories of my mother, Sylvia Miller Morris. I was 14 years old when my mother died of breast cancer, after less than a year of her diagnosis. My memories of her are a fuzzy blur of fixed photos that I have seen, as I suffered for years from traumatic memory loss. Although you may not have had traumatic memory loss, you possibly noticed one day that to feel the touch of your mother, remember the sound of her voice, or recall those special moments becomes just a little harder.

How often have you reached for the phone but forgotten that she wasn't there to answer? When was the last time you looked at the door waiting for her to come through but no one was there? How many times have you thought you just needed to hear her voice but there was nothing except silence? Are you missing your mother in a way that is bringing sadness, frustration, loneliness, and even anger? I've been there.

For years, I questioned myself as to why I could not remember her the way others remember their mothers. I know she loved me and I loved her, but those memories were lost, and I often felt responsible and even guilty for losing them. Just like that precious piece of jewelry, I was convinced for years that I was somehow responsible for losing something so significant to me.

"But one thing I do: forgetting what lies behind and straining forward to what lies ahead, I press on ..." (Phil. 3:13–14)

My life after the death of my mother became a press forward. You may feel this was a negative effect. I felt just that for many years. But looking back, knowing that our steps are really ordained by the Lord, I realized why the Lord allowed, and even ordained this period of isolation from memory.

My father, Bishop Ernest Morris, and my mother spent my childhood years working hard in order to establish and build the Mt. Airy Church of God in Christ (COGIC) ministry. My mother worked tirelessly, knocking on doors to promote Sunday school, cleaning the church before and after every service, creating and collating bulletins on Saturday night around the bed, as well as keeping finances and heading many ministries. Our church grew by leaps and bounds, adding more responsibility every day. In every obstacle we faced, the Lord showed Himself mightily to clear mortgages, move the congregation, and become a beacon of hope and salvation in the Germantown area.

Everything seemed perfect, I supposed, and then she was diagnosed with breast cancer. She died less than a year later despite prayers of support from around the nation. I actually do remember the day she died, when my father took my sister and myself to my aunt's house, then my uncle returned to the house announcing that she was gone. I recall a lot of sobbing and silent tears at times but that's all.

My next vivid memory was an audible recollection of my father crying at night. I could hear it through the walls of my bedroom. From that time on, I was determined to do whatever it takes to make sure my father finds joy. My own grief process became basically nonexistent as my memories were gone, and as I focused with my sister, Tanya, on making sure my father could be free to find love again. And he did find it with my "mother," Winifred Witherspoon Morris. Many were not able to understand our quick acceptance, but the thoughts of the Lord are not always the thoughts of man (Isa. 55: 8-9). God knows, God prepares, and God makes a way. We were able to bond together as a family, allowing my father and step mother to focus on the work of the Lord and continue the ministry. You can see the fruit of their labor clearly evident today. Surly, all things work together for the good (Rom. 8: 28).

Even the sad things work together for the joy of God's people.

Later in my life, I was blessed to meet and marry Elder Walter Chavers. Although we had admittedly a rocky start, we grew to understand and love each other very deeply. We worked together as partners in ministry to build our church's Youth Ministry. When he was diagnosed with stage four colon cancer, and given 6 months to live, I knew then the importance of spending time outside prayer saying, "good bye," not leaving a thing unsaid. I knew how to preserve that precious piece of memory so that it would not get lost. The example of my father's finding love again allowed me not to miss my love blessing in my husband, Samuel Greene Jr., whom I am sure God crafted and ordained for my life, and I for his. God equipped him for my sorrow and blessed us with a special gift, Gabrielle. Again, here is God's plan and purposes working together.

"In the secret of his tabernacle shall he hide me." (Ps. 27:5, KJV)

Ten years ago, I was diagnosed with breast cancer, exactly one year beyond the age my mother was diagnosed. I believe I was able to make the quick and concise choices for my own treatment without being paralyzed with fear because the Lord himself had shielded my memory against visions of my mother's illness. I did not dwell on suffering and dying; rather only on fighting and living. My blurred memory afforded me the ability to have razor focus on living. To God be the glory, I'm still here.

> *"I will restore to you the years that the swarming locust has eaten, the hopper, the destroyer, and the cutter."* (Joel 2:25)

Have you ever happened to find that precious piece that was previously lost long ago unexpectedly when you weren't looking for it? Just when it seems you have lost it forever your eye catches a glimmer. Could it be? Have I found it?

Over the past few years, I have begun rediscovering my mother, my precious piece. I am remembering her in so many ways even through the process of writing this chapter. I hear her voice during my conversations with my step mother. I see her organizational and leadership skills in my daughter, Stephanie, as she enhances everyone around her, and masters every challenge with resilience. I feel her heart of compassion for others as I see my son, Christopher, mentoring and as I hear him sharing his heart. I see her eyes in my daughter Gabrielle's eyes and I celebrate her ability to inspire as her grandmother once did. I see her in the mirror, looking at myself.

So, my discoveries continued by asking family members and friends to recall stories about her childhood and her adult life. I've renewed connections with women who worked with her in ministry. What was taken from me is now being restored in so many new ways. God is not only a healer, a savior, a forgiver, but He is a restorer. He restores our souls (Ps. 23:3).

Yes, there will be tears but God does dry our tears, and replaces them with rivers of joy. I'm trading my sorrow for the joy of the Lord. His joy is the strength we need to keep pressing forward without the physical presence of our natural mother (Neh. 8:10). If God cares about the little bird that is so minute in size and seemingly insignificant, how much more does He care about our thoughts, concerns, sorrows, and feelings of loneliness (cf. Matt. 6:26)? How much more does He want to comfort and bless us?

So, on this day I speak to you in your loss of your precious one. Although she is gone physically, be of good cheer she is not lost but found in everything around you.

You are God's daughter and He cares about you. Though for everything there is a season, and a time to mourn (Ecc. 3:1, 4), trust that the Lord will bring you out of this. We do not grieve as if we have no hope (1 Thess. 4:13). Wait in expectancy until the change comes. Wait in expectancy until you rediscover your precious mother. Wait in expectancy to be restored.

"Do not be anxious about anything, but in everything by prayer." (Phil. 4:6)

Today, I pray for you and your memory. I pray that every part of your precious piece be rediscovered in God's time. I pray that you will know that God makes no mistakes, and that He purposed our life to bless Him.

God reaches out to the inner parts of our sorrow and wipes away the tears of forgetting. The Lord is gracious, and full of compassion (Ps. 145:8, KJV). He is concerned about our grief and about us. Hear us Lord in the midnight hour of our grief. Weeping may tarry for the night, but joy comes with the morning (Ps. 30:5). Provide us with your joy. Help us wake up to a new day of restoration and discovery. Help us be purposeful in our restoration, and accepting of all we may find.

I pray for inner healing of loss feelings, for clear memories, and for new discoveries. Give us your peace, O Lord, as we press forward. Amen.

Words of Reflections

WHEN DOVES CRY

Chapter Two
There Is Joy in Your Mourning
By: Staci Morgan Boyd

"He heals the brokenhearted and binds up their wounds."

(Ps. 147:3)

February 14, 2008 marked for me what is commonly called a "milestone" birthday. You might think I would have been excited to turn 40. I had accomplished a lot. I had been through a lot: ups and downs, laughter and sorrows. And I had reached this significant point in my life you would think should set off the bells and whistles celebrating the new decade of life I was about to embark on.

But the bells and whistles didn't go off. My excitement was crippled by hearing that dreaded "C" word. That next chapter of my life was going to include the absence of my "hero." That next chapter was going to include so many milestones, and my mother wasn't going to be a part of them. She wasn't going to be physically here on earth to share them with me.

The day God had prepared me to celebrate 40 years of life ended up with me hearing, "your mother has stage 4 breast cancer and it is metastasizing." The cancer was spreading to other organs of her body. Those words echoed in my head over and over again. And instantly, I became numb. I felt like my heart just stopped beating. I stood there in complete devastation but could not show it. My mother kept a poker face. I wanted to shout, "Mom did you hear what she said?" I excused myself from the room; and there, outside the doctor's office, I found myself overcome with tears, hurt, and pain. Never did I ever expect this day would end up like this. I returned to the exam room in a pseudo self-composed state. My mother had the peace which surpassed all understanding (Phil. 4:7). But at that moment,

I could not join her in that peaceful state.

I couldn't process that I would be left here without the woman who gave me life. She sacrificed everything so that I could have the life experiences she didn't have. Who was going to help me raise my daughter? What was I going to do without the one person who had been there for me in every step of my life since I was in her womb? My number one role model wouldn't be there at my wedding. She wouldn't see my daughter graduating from 8th grade and moving on to High School. She wouldn't be here to see her go to her proms and graduate from High School. She would not see her go to college and graduate, like me. I couldn't stop thinking, "God, why? Why mom?"

My mother demonstrated an incredible level of strength. In the months that followed the diagnosis, she never showed fear. She never complained. She always spoke positively about her condition despite what the prognosis was. She even discussed getting a second opinion before going through treatment. She trusted and believed that God had the final say. I tried to follow her lead and be strong too. After all, my daughter was watching both of us. My mother always said, "Morgan ladies are strong." I understood her point; however, deep inside I wasn't feeling very strong. Thank God, He knows all our needs and provides for us even when we don't realize that we need Him (Matt. 6:8).

In the months that followed, my mom had good days and bad days. In March, I thought she was on her way to remission, but when April rolled around, her health began to decline. One more hospital stay and we received that call to come quickly to the hospital. You know it can't be good news when the call comes early in the morning, asking for you to come to the hospital right away. I had cried so much over the past few months that I didn't think I had any more tears left.

That phone call quickly reminded me that I still had more tears remaining. I made my way to the hospital on May 4, 2008. There, they told me there was nothing else that could be done medically for my mom, and that we needed to consider Hospice. I knew I needed to lift up my eyes to the hills to the Lord for strength and help (Ps. 121:1-2), because I wasn't going to make it on my own. My mom still had the peace that surpassed ALL understanding. My life was falling apart but she was calm. My heart was breaking but she still spoke of her faith. The doctor was truly an angel from God. She knew how to pray, and so she prayed as if God had told her exactly what to say. Thank God, for he knows all things. Our Father knows what we need even before we ask him (Matt. 6:8). And He provides, and never fails.

Everyone left the room except me. My mom told me to come and lie down beside her. I was 40 years old, but at that moment, I felt like I was a 4 years old child. My mom held me in her arms and told me she was ok with what God decided. She was at peace. She said she needed me to be that Morgan woman of strength. I tried to hear her words of encouragement but I couldn't. The tears flowed so heavy and so painfully that I couldn't breathe or speak.

My mom told me she was going to be ok. She said God is God and He does whatever He wills. He doesn't make mistakes. She was at that moment echoing the words of that great song, *"It is well with my soul."*[1] And in this she was wonderfully following our Lord's perfect example when He said to His Father, "Nevertheless, not my will, but yours, be done." (Luke 22:42). At that moment, I realized my mom was like that woman with the issue of blood in the Bible. She pushed her way through the crowds to touch the

---

[1] A hymn penned by hymnist Horatio Spafford and composed by Philip Bliss.

hem of the Lord's garment so that she would be healed (Luke 8:43-48). I realized that my mom did believe in God for her healing, and she was making her way to him for total and perfect healing. Only her healing would not be manifested here on earth but in heaven.

My mom wanted to be in her own bed, so we had home Hospice. It was a long week. My heart was so broken, but I took care of my mom as if she was going to be healed here on earth. The Hospice Care Manager told me her hearing would be the last to stop functioning, so I kept gospel music playing in her room. I read Scripture to her daily, and prayed without ceasing. God began speaking to me during her transition period. He told me she was ready to join Him, and I had to release her. He assured me that He will provide for me, that I will never be alone. I spoke to my spiritual mother on that Tuesday leading up to my mom's passing, and she confirmed what God had said. She told me that I had to tell my mom that I will be ok because she knew I would take her leaving very hard.

At that moment, my prayers changed. I prayed that God would make my mom's transition easier. I prayed that He would not allow her to suffer. If ever there was a time when I had to put my faith and trust in God, that was the time. I felt strength coming from the Lord. I began to experience the peace that my mom had, because I knew she was about to move into her mansion. She was about to walk on the streets of gold (Rev. 21). She wasn't going to have cancer anymore.

"Death shall be no more, neither shall there be mourning, nor crying, nor pain anymore."

(Rev. 21:4)

On Friday, May 9, 2008, my brother came and stayed with my mom, while my daughter and I got out of the house. After a while, he called, and told me that I needed to come home. I arrived home and headed directly to her room. I said, "Mom I'm here," and she took her last breath.

As I process this experience, I am reminded of the awesomeness of God. My mom was there when I took my first breath, and I was there when she took her last breath. What an example of Ecclesiastes 3:2! God has an eternal plan for everyone. Our job is to make sure we are in a right relationship with Him, so that His plan can go forth. Although the emptiness is still there without my mom, I know she is in a better place. I know that God doesn't make mistakes. He lets us know that life and death go hand in hand, but we don't need to be troubled because He will provide. He promised: "Behold, I am with you always, to the end of the age" (Matt. 28:20).

My mom's passing was definitely one of the hardest moments in my life. The reality that she would no longer be here for holidays and other significant events stayed on my mind constantly. What a tremendous emptiness in my heart! But I was reminded that God lost His only Son, so the truth is that God knew the loss, pain, and hurt I was experiencing having lost my only mother. In the days to come, He would be the ointment and the cure for my wounds. God's love and comfort would begin to heal my broken heart. Out of the tears and grief, I have grown so much in God. The tough yet comforting reality is that God always has the last say.

God has provided me with so many opportunities to help others who are going or have gone through this same experience. Let us not forget that we can lay our cares at the cross and trust God to carry them for us. For the Bible says, "For my yoke is easy and my burden is light" (Matt. 11:30), meaning we don't have to carry those heavy loads, including grief. God was faithful in His promise to watch over me after my mom had passed. And this Scripture became real for me during my healing process, "The Lord is near to the brokenhearted and saves the crushed in spirit" (Ps. 34:18). This reminds me daily that God is there for me. He knew my heart was broken, therefore, He sent the Comforter to comfort me (John 14:26).

When God called my mom home, this literally broke my heart. But I placed this heart that was in pieces in the perfectly capable hands of God in heaven. He put band aids on my broken heart, putting it back together. When God puts your broken heart back together, it will be brand new. Psalm 147:3 teaches us that God will put our broken hearts back together so that we could proceed with fulfilling His purpose and doing what we have been called to do despite our pain.

I want you to understand that you don't suffer alone. May be my loss is not the same as yours; however, the loss is still painful. It still leaves emptiness in our hearts. Know well that the storms of life are not hitting your life alone, it rather rains in everyone's life at some point. Just remember what Isaiah 61:1 says, "He has sent me to bind up the brokenhearted." Healing is a process that requires patience and time. God is an on-time God; He is never late; His timing is always perfect. When I thought about what was happening, I felt I was losing my mind, but God kept me safe in the midst of my storm.

Most gracious Father in heaven, hear my prayer. As I lift up my eyes to the hills for strength, I pray that You may touch the readers right now. Send Your healing power to mend their broken hearts. You can do anything but failing, so I am standing on Your Word. Your Word says that You will never leave us nor forsake us (Heb. 13:5). Your Word says, "blessed are those who mourn, for they shall be comforted" (Mat. 5:4). O Lord, Your Word says that there is a time for every matter under heaven (Ecc. 3:1), and this includes the loss of a loved one.

Lord, we know You have the final say in everything. I pray that You give us the strength to accept the things you allow to happen. You are the ultimate specialist for broken hearts. And while we understand that at times our hearts will be broken, we are totally confident that You will restore them anew. Thank you for sending us the Comforter, Your Spirit (John 14:26). Thank you for being a loving God. I pray that You comfort the readers, keep them in perfect peace, and shower down Your love from on high upon them. Restore their joy, that only you can do. Help them to know that joy does come with the morning (Ps. 30: 5). We are lifting up our eyes to the hills from where our help comes. In Jesus' Name, I pray. Amen.

WHEN DOVES CRY

*Words of Reflections*_____

WHEN DOVES CRY

Chapter Three
I Am The Gift She Left Behind
By: Julia D. Ford

"Suddenly, life has new meaning to me. There's beauty up above and things we've never taken notice of, you wake up and suddenly you're in love."

Such a great song by musical artist Billy Ocean. The Word of God, the comfort of the Holy Spirit, and these poetic lyrics were what I drew strength from during the time of my mother's SUDDEN death.

Tuesday morning, October 11, 2011 is a day I will always remember; that was the day my mother died. That morning, I received a text from my cousin saying my mother's boyfriend had called her, but he was crying and she couldn't understand a word. She asked if she could call him to gain some clarity about what was happening.

I excused myself from work and called my mother Madeline on her phone, her boyfriend answered the phone, and immediately called my name and kept saying, "Maddie is gone, Maddie is gone!" I thought he meant he and my mother had broken up, and his heart was grieving over it. My mother had a way of toying with his emotions just to get a laugh. He was sobbing, so I asked him to put someone else on the phone. Another woman took the phone from his hand to speak with me. She introduced herself to me as the ex-wife of my mother's boyfriend, "Listen, your mom is dead and her body is on the floor, what funeral home you want her to go to?" All I had expected was to call my mom and tell her to stop making her boyfriend emotional. "Your mom is dead…her body is on the floor, what funeral home should we take her body to?" Wait, lady, whom I don't even know, I never even knew you existed. Slow down on your words, you are taking me way too fast! "You WAKE UP and SUDDENLY!"

Suddenly; quickly; without warning; unexpectedly!

This is exactly what I thought and felt. As I was holding the phone, I replayed in my mind the events that just happened. I refused to allow myself some time to process the actual depth of the words. Rather than crying, the fixer one, the protector, and the one who gets to the bottom of everything aroused inside me and started to plan and organize. My response was not a boisterous yell asking for my mom to come on the phone as if this was a prank, nor was it soft silent tears falling down my face to make myself believe this call wasn't a cruel joke. I immediately accessed what was said and started to ask questions. "Why was her body on the floor?" She doesn't sleep on the floor. "Was she murdered?" She was fine when I spoke to her the day before. "Who else is in the house?" I wanted names and badge numbers. I let them know that I am her next of kin, and that I am not giving permission to anyone to remove her body until someone of legal authority tells me what happened. The police officer who had responded to the call told me what had taken place through the night. They were waiting for my call to give them permission to remove the body. I gave the needed permissions, got phone numbers for follow-up, then I had to begin the hardest task of my life: relaying my mother's death to all my family. When I hung up the phone I SUDDENLY realized that my life as I knew it had just CHANGED.

At the time when Maggie, the name my mother affectionately allowed me to call her, died, I did not allow myself time to mourn. I became hardened, and learned how to cope with my overbearing sadness. I simply began to work. And immediately, I called family and friends, and started to plan her memorial service. I instantly made the decision to cremate her due to lack of funds at that time. Oh yes, I shed a couple of tears when I had to create her obituary. I shed a few more tears when certain family members and friends came by to pay their respects. Although I had allowed myself brief moments to grief, I ultimately chose to go into "work mood." Work mood for me was to make sure everyone was ok, to counsel them, and to help them process all their feeling. I found myself helping everyone else with their grief when I was in fact in desperate need of the same counsel that I was providing. I felt so detached from my emotions during that time. I wouldn't say I was numb, but the process of me trying to figure out what was currently taking place left me feeling as if I wasn't a part of the loss of this incredible person. I felt like an outsider watching my own family struggling to get through the loss of my very own mother.

Some years before that, Maggie had moved to Georgia to be closer to her mom and other family members. So, I needed to prepare two memorial services for my mom, one in Georgia and the other in Philadelphia, in an attempt to help as many family members and friends as possible with the closure they needed due to her sudden death. When it was all said and done with, and after family members and friends had gone back home, and calls of condolences had slowed down, I still had not processed nor accepted my new reality. Maggie is no longer here with me.

If you had the chance to meet her, I know you would have loved her. She was funny, resourceful and very creative. If you love your meat blackened, then you would have definitely loved her cooking. Maggie had a quick mind, a contagious smile, and a forgiving heart. She would also have given you her last Rolo. I loved her benevolent spirit.

Some time has gone by now, a little over 5 years, to be exact. How am I doing? You may ask me. These 5 years have flown by and my tears have slowed down, and I can say that I am good. The process of accepting her death and the realization that this is permanent until we see each other again in heaven is still at times a hard pill to swallow.

For the last 5 years, I have felt like I was trapped in a bubble. Physically, I kept moving on. I assisted in Pastoring our church, I wrote books, co-hosted a radio program, mentored women, taught classes, and preached sermons, all the while being a wife and mother. But emotionally, I felt vulnerable. I felt as if all I had accomplished was still not enough to fill my emptiness. I was missing something, I was missing my mom, my cheerleader, my laugh partner. We had, Maggie and I, a unique relationship as a mother and daughter.

Due to mom's previous years of drug abuse, we had exchanged roles. I had become the mother and she became the daughter; not in age or in title but in responsibility. This silent power transition did not occur overnight, but rather through a series of events related to her decision making while under the influence of drugs and alcohol.

On one such occasion, my mother, my sister and I were evicted from our apartment. Maggie had not paid the rent for a few months. She used the money to support her drug habit rather than taking care of the rent, food, and utilities. During a conversation, she and I had, she agreed that our housing issue was due to her poor financial management. She admitted that she used the funds on everything other than her responsibilities. My mother knew she had a drug problem, and was in need for help to get clean at least on that day. She promised to get her life back together, and promised to do better for the sake of my sister and me. But I had heard that speech several times before, and things somehow seemed to go right back to the way it was.

I finally realized I had to do something, so I got a job. This job was of great help for my sister and me, and also for the new place we moved into. I chose to step up into the provider's role, while my mother concentrated on her financial scheme so that she could get next fix. I was perfectly fine with stepping up to do the job my mother wasn't capable of doing, and my mother was ok with having less responsibilities. This allowed my sister and me to have at least food on a regular basis.

Towards the end of Maggie's life, our relationship became one of daily talks over the phone, catching up on the latest family and celebrity gossips. Maggie wanted to know the latest happenings in my children's lives, my church, and between my husband and me. She always wanted to help me and my family out. She even tried to convince me to hire her as an au pair for my kids, and housekeeper "slash" cook for my entire family, as she would say with a giggle in her voice. She loved my three children with all she had, they gave her the air she needed to breathe again. Many times, being a grandparent is a parent's second chance to get it right again through grandchildren. It's like a fresh start for all the mistakes the parents made with their own kids. If it were one place my mother felt safe, this place was in the eyes of my children, her grandchildren. Through our daily conversations, our relationship started to heal and she started to thrive.

It's usually at the end of life that one realizes how important their decisions and life choices were to what they are going to leave behind. Maggie did not live a spotless life, most of us don't. Yet, I am quite sure that if she had a chance to do it all over again, she would delete some scenes from her drama-filled life. Maybe she didn't cross every "T" or dotted every "I," but she did take me to church. And it was through having a relationship with God, and attending his house of faith that I learned how to forgive and why. It felt good to be forgiven by God, so I wanted to do the same for others, especially my mom, obeying God's command, "Be kind to one another, tenderhearted, forgiving one another, as God in Christ forgave you" (Eph. 4:32).

Once I had forgiven my mom for the years of hurt and pain she caused during her several years of addiction, I experienced a newly-found freedom and peace. It was then that I could see her good side rather than focusing on all her wrongs. It's the enemy's job to make you see only hurt, pain, and rejection in those close to you. I chose to get rid of everything I considered to be my mother's wrongdoings against me and against our family. I took a conscious decision to release her from the pain that she had caused me. I simply decided not to hate her anymore.

When I took this step, a new world of acceptance and appreciation began. I began to see my mother's good qualities coming through me especially in the way I parent my own children. I thank the Lord for the opportunity I had to get closure in this area of my life while she was still alive. It's funny, I never saw forgiveness as a closure, I just wanted to move on from that place of brokenness. It was a blessing to have peace with my mother prior to her death.

Are you struggling with open-ended situations between you and your mom that were not resolved prior to her death? My counsel for you is to forgive yourself, then go and clear the air between you and your children as best as you can. Let's not leave anything open-ended with our own children. Let's not pay our pain forward.

Remembering Maggie's great qualities brings healing to my mind and spirit. And if I don't try to find the good things in and through her life, the bad thoughts about her and her actions will then become the pacifier I will always depend on to help put me to sleep. Pastor Shirley Caesar sang it best, "I remember momma in a happy way." Can you join me in remembering your momma in a good and happy way?

Maggie left her good qualities behind on this earth. She left me, my sister, and the next generation, my children, behind. She had an ability to decorate any space on a dime. I too am able to do the same. She had a profound sense of humor that could bring you out of any dark place. I too am able to go into the dark places of people's minds and inject the gift of laughter.

Some things, beloved, are taught while others are caught. I caught a lot just by being Madeline's daughter. All that was good about her life was her gift to this world. She loved me and told me so. Every time we spoke she said how much she adored me. She believed I could fly. She believed that whatever life throws in my way, I can rise above it. Maggie said once that anything she didn't get right, my sister and I would make it right through our lives and accomplishments. I am now ready to embrace that I AM THE GIFT THAT SHE LEFT BEHIND. This gift is that kind of gifts that keeps on giving; for it was my job to demonstrate all my mother's great traits to my kids. And it's up to me to encourage them to teach their own children the same, and so on and on.

My sincere prayer for you today is that you too will find healing after your mother's death. I pray that you no longer see yourself through your mother's failures. I speak that the generational curses that have tormented you shall be broken in JESUS' NAME. I speak that your vision shall be clear in order to see the good in your mother's life. I speak that you shall embrace that you are the best thing she could ever have accomplished in this world.

I also pray for your heart, for this emptiness in the pit of your stomach. I release you in the name of Jesus from rejection, hurt, shame, guilt, and embarrassment. I release a new day to be your portion. I speak that the true love of Christ shall enter your heart and mind, and override all negative thoughts and debates. I speak that you shall live for the better as you make your journey down the road of healing. I shut the mouth of every evil word spoken over your life. You are more than a conqueror (Rom. 8:37), and your best days are still ahead of you in Jesus' name. I release the love of the Lord to be the healing balm your heart needs. I believe the Greater One (1 John 4:4) who is in you, who is Christ Jesus, will bring this prayer to pass, in Jesus' Name I pray, AND IT IS SO!

*Words of Reflections*_____

WHEN DOVES CRY

Chapter Four
It's Never Too Late
By: Roneve Davis

On January 2011, I received a phone call from my mom. She was at that time living in Jamaica, West Indies, where she was born. She had retired there almost twelve years before that, in a beautiful house she had worked very hard to build. "I'm sick," she said, "and none of the doctors in Jamaica can figure it out." My response was, "MA!!!! Why are you messing around with those doctors? You are a Unites States citizen with Medicare, please get up and come here right away, and let's go to some real doctors (no offense to doctors in Jamaica, what I meant was that the doctors in the U.S. have more experience. I'm going to get myself all hemmed up telling you my whole story). Anyway, I told my mother to come back to New York and see her Primary Care physician to find out what was wrong. My mom had always been a full-figured woman weighing about 220 lbs. She neglected to tell me that she had been down to 160 lbs due to this sickness.

Now, a background on my relationship with my mom: We were not close. My mom was not close to any of her children. She had three; me, my brother and my sister. For as long as I can remember, we rarely saw her as she worked a lot; and as long as I can remember, she had a bad habit of gossiping badly about her children. She did talk badly about us. When we were younger, if we got 5 As and one F, everyone would hear about the F, and nothing about the As. This is just the way she was. This made us not to want much to do with her.

There were also times she lied on us. I remember hearing her, when we were younger, talking on the phone, and lying on one of us. We would look at each other as if we were saying, "What is she talking about?" People often looked at me and my siblings as if we were so terrible for not having a close relationship with our mother, but we were hurt by her actions, and we were the only ones who knew that truth. I used to call my mom on her birthday, Mother's Day, Thanksgiving, Christmas and New Year's, and may be once or twice to say "hi." Did she love me?

Yes, and I loved her too, but we were just not close.

My mom took my advice and went to her Primary Care physician in New York around February 2011. Her doctor admitted her to the hospital for evaluation, and she spent a few weeks there. My brother, who lives in New York, was the one able to speak on her behalf. When the hospital was unable to come up with a diagnosis, they discharged her. She was still sick and not getting any better. So, she went to a well-known hospital in Manhattan, where she was admitted. They ran a series of tests, and had many specialists examine her case, but still were unable to come up with a diagnosis. At this point, my mom was down to approximately 110 lbs. She was discharged then to my cousin's house, and by that time she was hardly walking.

During that time, I was working as a Marketing Director for a skilled nursing facility in Delaware; and this is exactly what my mom was in desperate need of. I managed to get a room for her inside the facility. My brother furnished a bed in the back of his SUV, laid my mom back there, and we met on the NJ Turnpike where I picked up my mom and laid her in the back of my car. She was so weak my brother had to carry her in his arms and put her into my car. I drove her straight to the facility where she was admitted. This was in late August 2011.

My mom's admission to the facility I worked for was a pivotal point in our relationship. I made sure she got the best physical and occupational therapy possible. At that time, my husband worked for a Gastroenterology group known to be the best in this field. So, we had all my mom's records sent to them for evaluation. During that time, I got to see my mom daily, and we shared some very funny moments when she was still with me, and that was good.

I remember two wonderful extra special moments with my mom when she was still there with me. This is the first one: One day I was talking on the phone with my brother, and he asked me, "Is mom saved?" I said, "Hmmm, I don't know." He said, "Well, you better find out." I said, "Ok." Then I went into my mom's room and said, "Mommy, are you saved?" She answered, "I don't know." I said, "Well, we are going to take care of that right now." I then walked her through a salvation prayer that she said so heartfully. I said, "Now you are saved." I gave her a hug. She looked at me and said, "Thank you." I told her my brother helped as well, wanting her to acknowledge him too. She said, "Well, thank you both."

The other significant moment was that one day while I was sitting at my desk, I heard the Lord telling me, "Go tell your mother you love her." I put my pen down as if saying, "Come on Lord! Stop giving me hard stuff to do!" I know this seems surprising, but I couldn't even remember one time we ever told each other that. I say it every day to my husband and children, but I found it extremely difficult to say it to my mother.

As my mom was staying in my facility, I was typically able to see her often. After I got off at 4:30pm, I would go and spend time with her in her room. On the day that I was told to say, "I love you" to her, I remember sitting there with her for hours not knowing how to say it. I knew I couldn't leave the room until it was done. I had to obey. "Why was this so hard?" I thought to myself. Then, I got up and gave her a hug and said quickly: "I Love you," and she right away said, "I Love you too," as if she had been busting to say it her entire life. I walked out and sat in my car, breathing as if I had been chased, and thought to myself, "she has always wanted to tell me that." That day started the "I Love you" frenzy. We wouldn't hang up the phone, nor leave each other without saying it, as if we were trying to catch up on a life time of "I Love you's." It was a great moment in our relationship.

My mom was discharged from the facility at the end of November 2011. She stayed first at my home, which she said was very nice. I even overheard her telling one of her friends that my home was very nice, and I remember smiling because she was saying something nice about me. After this short stay, the Home Health nurse told us that my mom needed to go back to the hospital. My husband and I drove her to the biggest hospital in Delaware, where the doctors that my husband worked for were affiliated.

I kept fasting and praying until my mother was diagnosed. I did not eat solid food, only liquids. I visited my mom every day after work. I didn't let her know I was fasting. I remember one day I was walking into the hospital, and she said, "The doctors found out what was wrong with me, they ordered a bone marrow which confirmed the diagnosis." I said, "Are you sure?" I went and asked the nurse, she confirmed that they in fact had a diagnosis. And immediately, I took the crackers on my mom's overbed table, and ate them like a vicious animal. Mom said, "Wow! You're hungry!" I told her then about the fasting I had been on for two weeks. She said, "You did that for me?" I said, "You couldn't eat so neither could I." I remember her being touched by that. At this point, my mom was down to about 99 lbs.

My mom had a house in Georgia, and my sister lived about 10 minutes from there. Mom wanted to go there for recuperation. I took her by plane to Georgia in March

2012 and arranged Home Health aides, Physical Therapy, Occupational Therapy, and Nurses for her. She started TPN, a way of feeding through veins. She also started chemotherapy. My sister took over from there. I saw hope of recovery.

During that time, I spoke often to my mom, and my family and I went to visit her in August 2012. On November 20, 2012, my mom was admitted to the hospital in Georgia for what I thought was just a minor setback. On November 26, 2012, my sister called and said mom was not doing well, and whether we should put her on hospice or not. I thought we should as I was familiar with their services.

On November 27, 2012, I received a phone call at 5am. The woman on the other line said, "Your mom is gone." I sat straight up in the bed and said, "WHAT??!!" She said, "Your mom is gone." I asked, "Is this the hospital?" The woman said, "No, I'm calling from the Hospice center; your mom was transferred here last night." I asked her to tell me what my mom's mood and atmosphere were; she told me that she was staying in a private room, lights were down, soft music playing, with her Bible opened. And she had gone peacefully during sleep, with a sigh of relief. I told her we would be in touch as she would be transferred to New York.

My mom's home-going ceremony was exactly the way she would have wanted it. My brother covered all expenses sparing nothing; he did everything with excellence and did not skimp on anything. All of her grandchildren wore white, because they were the light of her life. I was so happy for her because of the end she had had.

All this changed the day after the funeral. My sister informed me of something my mom told her about my brother and me which was a big malicious LIE. My months of love turned into hatred. She hadn't changed a bit! I was so mad, fuming with disgust, extremely mad that I couldn't overcome it. Being mad at someone who has passed away is very difficult because you cannot tell them, so it becomes an internal turmoil.

God began to work with me on forgiveness, but I didn't want to forgive her because she was a liar. However, this unforgiveness began to eat at me daily, and I couldn't shake it. I remember one time I entered a room alone, and I started yelling at her, asking her why she lied on us the way she did, and why she wanted to hurt her own children. After I finished yelling and getting it all off of my chest, I said, "I forgive you, I forgive you, I forgive you." And I fell on the floor, weeping.

Still on the floor, God, the Good Shepherd (John 10:11) and the Potter (Jer. 18), took me on a journey, showing me my mom as a single mother working and working. He showed me Christmas, and a house full of presents, though she wasn't there because she had to work a double job. Yet, we always had abundance of toys. He showed me myself and my siblings dressed in uniforms because we went to private schools. He showed me plenty of food and snacks. Never were we denied a hearty lunch at school. He also showed me the beautiful house my mom bought for us in Long Island, my car, and the college she sent me to. Then He said, "Would a mother who did not have love in her heart do all of this for you?" I got up and said, "Thank you, Mommy, thank you so very much." From that moment on, my forgiveness and love developed more and more. This journey into the sanctuary of God was very fruitful (Ps. 73:17). So, I got a framed picture of my mom, and I now think back of my childhood with gratefulness filling my heart. I chose to remember only the positive things about my mother, not the negative things. My relationship with her became better than it has ever been. You may say it's a little late, but I say it's never too late.

I hope this has been a blessing to you. I know it's not your traditional warm and fuzzy mom stories, nonetheless, it is mine. And my mom and I are now closer to each other than we have ever been.

In My Heart,

God bless you all.

*Words of Reflections*_____

WHEN DOVES CRY

Chapter Five

The Goodness of the Lord
by: Andrea Riley

"I would have fainted, had I not believed to see the goodness of the LORD in the land of the living!"

(Psalm 27:13)

With assuredness and confidence, mom would recite this adage derived from Psalm 27:13, one of her favorite Scriptures.

What a unique soul, who definitely marched to a different beat! My mom brought her own style of music to everything she touched. Her melodious spirit radiated creativity, joy, strength, and grace. Her beautiful heart was the only thing that surpassed her beautiful appearance.

Dare I say she was the epitome of perfection? Not at all, and she would be okay with that. Mom was that type of person who would allow people to be humans; and who would still be loved in spite of flaws, imperfections, and shortcomings.

Now for a little background: I was my mom's first born. She never wanted girls because she hated doing hair. Over the years, my thick, kinky locks reinforced her belief that she was right in wishing for boys. During that time, I also had my share of occasions when I wished for a different mother.

As a young child, I was absolutely and unapologetically a daddy's girl. My youthful eyes viewed my father as a fun-loving and playful man. But for the most part, I viewed my mom as impatient and irritable. She used to comment on how I was always frowning, and I used to wonder why she would fuss and get upset over the least little thing. So, although we both LOVED each other, we didn't necessarily LIKE each other that much.

My parents separated when I was ten. My brothers and I moved from Philadelphia into a rural part of Virginia to live with our eighty-something years old great-great grandmother. Mom worked at a nursing home that was thirty miles away, where she also resided during week days. She would visit us in most weekends. My opinion of her didn't change much during that period. And from what I could tell, that was mutual.

The following year, we moved into our own apartment in Richmond. And there, our relationship took a dramatic turn. As the eldest child, I stepped up and assumed responsibility in many areas. That was when I began to understand how hard my mother worked and how exhausted she felt at the end of her nursing shift. Therefore, I started looking for ways to help lightening her load. It amazed me to see how much a tuna sandwich and a bowl of soup could make her day and lift her spirit up; and how a catnap could refresh her and unleash her kind and gentle side. Our appreciation for one another grew by leaps and bounds. I discovered that she was hilarious (This was significant for me, because I LOVE to laugh). For the first time, she was delighted in having a daughter. Even more than mother and daughter relationship—we became friends.

Over the next few years, our bond got strengthened. She became my favorite "cut-up buddy." We could talk about almost anything. My responsibilities in the household increased and they included being her official sounding board. She knew she could count on me. And I did my best not to let her down.

Things went well between us for a number of years. Eventually, we moved to Atlanta. For the first time, we stayed in a place I loved more than my native Philly. I was overjoyed about this transition. Life was great for some time; that is, until my senior year at High School. The summer before that, my mom met a man, and they started dating. In the early stages of the relationship, I was happy for her. He said and did all the right things to sweep her off her feet. It was good seeing her so joyful. There was no way either of us could have foreseen the impending devastation.

Once this boyfriend moved into our home, his true colors began to surface. Not before long, it became evident to me that he was a wolf in sheep's clothing. His strategy was to divide and conquer. And he accomplished this through planting negative seeds against me. My mom then began saying and doing things that were totally out of character. This prompted me to isolate myself in my bedroom in order to avoid conflict. Within few weeks, our close-knit relationship was completely deteriorated to the point that we rarely spoke to each other. Once he had succeeded in putting a distance between my mother and me, he made his big move. One day he asked why I locked my bedroom door at night. The following day, he manipulated mom into removing my door off its hinges, under the pretext of preventing me from isolating myself from the family. At that point, I knew it was time for me to flee and go live with my father.

Fearing retaliation, I left the impression that I was going to visit dad during Christmas break. Once out of harm's way, my father and I confronted her. A personality, which was clearly not my mother's, spoke hateful things against me, and said the family was better off without me. The influence of a different spirit was clearly evident. Things got so ugly that she refused to send me my clothes or school records.

The ensuing chain of events led me to a period of anger, resentment, and depression. It felt as though my life had been flipped upside down, with no fault of my own. In retaliation, I cast the most unfavorable light possible upon my mother; sharing tainted versions of stories with relatives with every bit of malice, spite, and vindictiveness I could muster.

Little did either of us realize at that time, but actually we were both mourning. We were grieving over the loss of a mother, a daughter, and a friend. And in our pain, our hearts grew cold and callous towards each other.

Ironically, this was the same person who instilled in me not to be catty, vicious, hateful, petty, vengeful, or backbiter. Now, both teacher and student were displaying these distasteful and loathsome traits. Desire and sin beget death (Jam. 1:15). We were spiritually dead; and the wages of sin is death.

However, the free gift of God is eternal life in Christ Jesus our Lord (Rom. 6:23)! Thank God for that truth that became my reality one week before my twentieth birthday. The heavy burden of sin over my head had been lifted up (Ps. 38:4; 32:5). Having been forgiven much, I also loved much (Luke 7:47). The One who forgave me released me to forgive all who had hurt me, including my mom. He reconciled me to himself through Christ, and gave me the ministry of reconciliation to extend towards others (2 Cor. 5:18-19). I was able to let go of past hurts, because the Lord revealed to me who my true enemy was: Satan; for we do not wrestle against flesh and blood (Eph. 6:12). Mom had done and said bad things to me while under his evil influence. This same devil had lured me into sinning against her, as well. With this newly-found freedom, I began interceding for my entire family, mom included.

Over time, mom was able to forgive the hurt she felt

because of the way I had left. I rejoiced greatly when she made the decision to rededicate her life to Christ. Not only did God heal us, he also wiped away our scars. Once restored, we became closer than ever. We became not simply best friends, but we also prayer partners.

Years later, during her early fifties, an illness attacked my mom's body. She continued to work for long, hard days, rarely missing it. At one point, her balance was off, and she started experiencing dizzy spells. At that time, her job was more than an hour away; and she became so ill that she often had to stop along the way to gather herself before continuing her daily commute. But she kept pressing on to work every day.

There was another period when her breathing was belabored, and in addition she had an exhaust problem that caused fumes to pour into her car. When this happened, mom only rolled down her window and kept going to work. Through it all, she demonstrated a level of perseverance not many can attain.

As even the most solid rock gradually erodes over time due to constant exposure to wind and rain, so it was with mom's body due to the continual exposure to her ailment. Although this chronic condition wreaked havoc in her body for more than twenty years, it couldn't extinguish her sense of humor, fun-loving nature, and indomitable spirit.

Just as seasons change, there comes a juncture in one's life when tables turn and the adult child assumes the role of the encourager, the exhorter, and the caretaker. I can't say that I saw this coming. It feels as if one day I was receiving instructions from her; and the next one I was giving her directives. And without realizing, I used the selfsame principles she had instilled in me to admonish her. Not sure when this happened, but the script had somehow flipped. The woman who had astonished me with a seemingly endless flow of creativity became the one who would marvel at my inventiveness. Not sure WHEN or HOW it happened, I just know that it DID happen. God surely has a way of surprising us.

We spent the last three years of mom's life on a weekly prayer call with a group of intercessors, praying for our adult children. As with most things she was committed to doing, mom was so very faithful, rarely missing a call. There were times she was sick or even hospitalized, yet she remained devoted to interceding for others.

Mom became severely sick in January of last year that her doctors expected she would require round-the-clock care upon release from the hospital. I arranged to fly down to her for several weeks to be at her side until she got back on her feet. But she made such a remarkable recovery that I planned to return home a week earlier than anticipated. The physicians were shocked during her follow up visits to see how well she fared!

Just when we had begun to breathe a sigh of relief, mom got ill once again. She was hospitalized a few weeks later, on Easter Sunday. Her children and husband gathered at her bedside, watching the life support apparatus aggressively blasting air into her lungs, her lips chapped, and her face swollen. We all knew it was time to let go. She'd fought a long, hard–but valiant–battle. She'd finished the race, kept the faith. When the plug was pulled, we sang, prayed, and said our goodbyes. I had no regrets, because there was nothing left unsaid. No kind deeds left undone.

We later honored her by fulfilling two outstanding wishes for her—a virtual memorial service, and a family legacy book recording her family tree for the generations to come. Here is an excerpt of my tribute in her book:

> *Mom,*
> *When people say that I am just like you, I receive it as the highest compliment. Thank you so very much for all the wonderful things you have instilled in, as well as modeled before me. The short list*

includes:
Appreciation, Artistic Ability, Boldness, Character, Commitment, Consideration, Courage, Creativity, Dependability, Diligence, Endurance, Entrepreneurial Spirit, Faith, Friendship, Generosity, Gratefulness, Honesty, Humor, Ingenuity, Integrity, Intelligence, Laughter, Leadership, Longsuffering, Love, Loyalty, Outside-the-Box Thinking, Patience, Prayer, Responsibility, Strength, Strong Work Ethic, Supportiveness, Thoughtfulness, Truthfulness, Uniqueness, and Wisdom. Your care for me over the years made it my honor and privilege to take care of you in your time of need. You were there to welcome me into the world when I took my first breath ... and I was blessed to be present to bid you farewell as you took your last breath. Until our reunion in heaven, you will live on in my heart.

-Your devoted daughter Andrea

As I write this chapter, I realize that my story is neatly packaged. Everything seems to have come together perfectly for my mother and me, and for this I am grateful. Yet and still, my heart goes out to this daughter whose relationship with her mother did not end on a positive note. For those who may be experiencing negative emotions of regret, shame, anger, resentment, disappointment, depression, self-pity, sadness, loneliness, inadequacy, rejection, or confusion—I feel your pain.

The good news is that the same God, who healed our situation back then, is more than enough to heal yours now. For He is the Father of lights, with whom there is no variation (Jam. 1:17). Our hope came through reliance on Christ and His shed blood to wash away our sins. His power and His love were what wrought miracles in us. He enabled us to forgive each other–and just as importantly–to forgive ourselves. If you just ask Him, He will freely provide you with eternal life, healing, freedom from the past, and hope for the future. *"For we can do all things through Him who strengthens us"* (Phil. 4:13).

Here's a suggestion for any daughter who misses her mother, or perhaps who wishes she had done more while she was still alive. Try creating a legacy book for her. I chronicled my mother's life in pictures from her birth through her golden years. I collected loving words, special tributes, and fond memories from anyone who wanted to take part. The book included pictures of every relative and friend I could find. Creating this book for my mother was a cure for me. When I miss her, I pull it out and look through it. It continues to bless me each time I open it.

I believe this book will minister to anyone who would honor her mother this way. Keep in mind that the blessing is not in how elaborate or detailed the book is—the blessing is in the process itself of creating a lasting gift in her memory.

I will leave you with this prayer of comfort.

Father, I pray for every daughter who is reading this chapter. I pray that she would come to know you as the Father of mercies, and the God of all comfort. For you are the one who comforts her in all her affliction (2 Cor. 1:3-4).

Jesus, you said you would not leave her comfortless, and you would come to her (John 14:18; KJV). Come to your daughter, right now. Let her feel your presence; for in your presence, there is fullness of joy (Ps. 16:11).

Father, give her beauty for ashes, the oil of joy for mourning, the garment of praise for the spirit of heaviness (Isa. 61:3; KJV). May she turn to you when she is weary and heavily laden, so you can give her rest (Matt. 11:28).

Teach her to lay every burden, weight, hardship, grievance, trouble, and regret at your feet.

For every daughter experiencing guilt or shame I pray, Isaiah 55:7 promises that if she returns to you, that you will have compassion on her, and you will abundantly pardon her. Help her to forgive herself.

For the daughter who is experiencing rejection I pray, Psalm 27:10 says that even if her father or mother forsake her, the Lord would take her in. Jesus, you were despised and rejected by men; you have borne her grief and carried her sorrows (Isa. 53:3-4), making her accepted in the beloved (Eph. 1:6). I pray that your daughter would see the goodness of the Lord in the land of the living, in Jesus' name. Amen.

Words of Reflections

WHEN DOVES CRY

Chapter Six

Heaven Bound

By: Jennifer Marlowe

Her name is Myrtle Adassa Cox, affectionately known as "Mama" or "Madda (Mother) Murks." She was born in 1928 in a small village called Clonmel, St. Mary in Jamaica. Myrtle was a single mother of five kids, one boy and four girls. Even though she had little education due to sickness at an early age, this didn't stop her from providing for her children. She was a workaholic, strong, black woman whose heart was as big as the universe. With the little she had, her household welcomed everyone. It always seemed as if she had *just* enough for everyone regardless of their journey.

Mama was also a woman of prayer; a prayer warrior, whose head was always covered or tied with her prayer shawl. Even on her deathbed, she had her head covered. Being full of substance and character, she taught her children that it is better to be respected than to be liked. Madda Murks taught me how to be my best self. She showed me how to influence people and lead them to God; how to be comfortable in my skin and fully committed to the love and responsibility God has given me. I found this lady to be amazingly strong and resiliently dignified. Surely these wonderful words apply to her, that with the virtuous woman: "Strength and dignity are her clothing, and she laughs at the time to come. She opens her mouth with wisdom, and the teaching of kindness is on her tongue" (Prov. 31:25, 26). *This woman was my mother!*

I recall one time I was sitting on my mother's bedside holding her hand, uncomfortably fighting back tears. It was as if my tears were battling the sorrow of my heart, fighting to pour behind my hazel eyes; the same colored eyes that I inherited from this woman.

She asked, "Paulette," a nickname mama endearingly used to address me by.

"Yes mama," I answered.

"Am I going to be like this for the rest of my life?" "Like what?" I asked. She gripped my hand as if yearning for security and whispered, "Not remembering things."

At that moment, I did what I had learned to do over the last few months since the cancer returned more aggressively; I cried with no sound. I had become an expert in silent sobs. I had learned to let tears flow like water without a whimper or a sound of heart breaking. It hurt so much because my mother was usually so good at remembering things. She was my human calendar. She would remind me of appointments, dates, and all things that I needed to get done. Sometimes, she would tease me saying she should "send me to the doctors to check on my brain." Now here she is, this woman… my mama… my mother, slumbering, not knowing even where she was. But it is okay; I knew my God was going to heal her, for "He was pierced for our transgressions; He was crushed for our iniquities; upon him was the chastisement that brought us peace, and *with his wounds we are healed*" (Isa. 53:5).

Fourteen years before my mom's death, she was diagnosed with a cancerous tumor in her intestines. She ended up having a major surgery, where half of her intestines had to be removed. As her recovery process after the surgery was so long and agonizing, she told her children never to let her have another surgery again, if her cancer returned. She was adamant about this too. So, when mom began to get sick, and all the symptoms looked familiar, we knew the cancer was back. And after everything was medically confirmed, we, her children, decided what was best for our mother. We promised to give her the best care and attention for the rest of her days. We shared in the process of taking care of our mother. Mama would be home-cared for by her second youngest daughter, while the rest of her children would financially support them both.

Everything was settled physically, but emotionally, I wasn't in a good state of mind; I was a wreck. This illness meant death, and that's why fear crept in. *"Fear and trembling came upon me, and horror overwhelmed me"* (Ps. 55:5). Fear was brash and unsolicited, and it spoke so loud if felt deafening, "Your mama, your mother, is going to die!" So, here I am frightened, panicking, with the spirit of uncertainty aiming to paralyze my faith. Why did this monstrous disease have to return? Why did this lovely, beautiful, and righteous woman must fight twice? I know the Bible says: *"God sends rain on the just and on the unjust"* (Matt. 5:45), but why did this rain have to fall upon my family? It is said that the storms of life come to teach us something, but I wasn't in the mood to be a student; nor ready to learn anything new.

We knew then what the disease was: it is of the demon; the demon is that which cancer is. Therefore, we knew how to pray. I am a part of an awesome prayer ministry. We've prayed for hundreds of people, and we've witnessed people being healed, delivered, and set free. "So why worry?" I asked myself. When we prayed for mama, we intuitively applied the same methods of fasting and praying, decreeing and declaring, binding and loosening, making declarations and claiming our rights. Moreover, we believed that God would remember mama's faithfulness, as she was also part of the prayer ministry. I had no doubt she was going to be healed; but when, that I didn't know. I patiently waited for the healing to be manifested. I believed in the Word and I had faith.

Even when my mom was weak, she would slowly make her way down the stairs to the prayer room in the basement of our house, each Saturday evening. Mamas always found her in the midst of great prayers. When shouts were going up, unflinching and joyful, she found herself right where the presence of God would show up. Her body would start to shake under the power of the anointing and she would speak in tongues. I believe that in those moments, my mother would have a conversation with Jesus. She would go through a deep exchange, beseeching a promise for her healing. Fatefully that was my hope, for it is said in Matthew 18:19 *"Again I say to you, if two of you agree on earth about anything they ask, it will be done for them by my Father in heaven."*

As the days, weeks, and months passed, mama got weaker and her pain grew worse. She ate less and regressed more. The doctors decided it was time for hospice care, and morphine was prescribed to help with her pain. We were hoping that the medication would make her life more peaceful, and that she would be in less agony. But one of my sisters and I disagreed about that with the rest of our siblings because we thought taking this medicine would actually shorten her life span. However, we soon realized that we were being selfish, never comprehending that mama's pain was greater than our needs. I admit we selfishly wanted mama here with us as long as possible, but we soon recognized that our care and love for this great woman should supersede our wishes. We had to meet her needs.

One evening after work, I instinctively took my usual place of lying beside my mother, beside her weak and frail body. She slightly opened her eyes and asked, "Who is that?" I replied, "It's me, Paulette." She smiled and closed her eyes. In the stillness of the room, I could hear her faint breathing, and I thought to myself, "YES! We have been granted another day." For me, that became a precious commodity; that meant Life.

Giving mama a bath became for me a comfort and a privilege. She was a little uneasy, and I could see in her eyes a bit of embarrassment, but I could also see that she was physically relaxed and content, because she was in the comfort of her daughters' care. Her wish was being granted, and she was alert enough to know that we had done what she asked of us. When she could not eat solid food anymore, it became puréed, and we even took turns in feeding her.

During those times, we had our own individual conversations with her about any and every thing. She was particularly interested in the updates about church. You see, my mama *loved* going to church. Even when she was sick and in pain, she tried to convince us she could make it to church. Ironically, I gained a sense of humor during my mama's time of sickness. I told all kinds of jokes. I remember her laughing and saying, "What am I going to do with you, child?" At that time, I never realized this was my way of dealing with her illness. I simply thought it was my natural reaction, wanting to make her happy and laugh. I always wanted to remember her smiling and in good spirit. "It's okay," I convinced myself, "the healing might take a while to manifest but I trust God." For it is written in Nehemiah 8:10 *"Then he said to them, "Go your way. Eat the fat and drink sweet wine and send portions to anyone who has nothing ready, for this day is holy to our Lord. And do not be grieved, for the joy of the LORD is your strength."*

I distinctively remember a conversation we had had when she asked why this "thing had to come back," and why did it have to attack her body? She said she had been searching herself to see if she had done anything wicked, asking God to bring back to her memory anything she might have done and not asked for repentance for it. What was it that may have attached itself to her? She wanted to repent now while her mind was still functioning. I consoled her by saying, "No, mama, it's just an attack planned by the enemy. But God is going to heal you!" I told her that because my faith was that extraordinary, and that was what I truly believed. Then, trying to lighten the atmosphere, I took my mother's hand and laid it over my head. I tried to play out the Jacob and Esau story. Laughing, I said, "Bless me, mama. I want my sisters' birthright." She laughed with her eyes closed, implying she was amusingly shaking her head at me. Then she smiled and said, "I'll pray for you anyhow." And she *did*.

There were other days when I would walk into her room, and I could hear her singing in a faint voice, worshiping her King. During one of her praise and worship sessions in bed, I joined her in singing, *"we are standing on holy ground and I know that there are Angels around, let's just praise Jesus now, because we are standing on holy ground."* I could see tears streaming down her cheeks, and the light of glory shining on her face. "Oh, mama," I cried silently, "I love you, don't leave me now."

A few weeks later, mama stopped walking, talking, and eating; her only position was sleep. All of us could see mama's end drawing near. Her son, daughters, and grandchildren came from different states, and as a family, we were all there. While I could hear family and friends chattering downstairs, I walked into mom's room like I did each evening. Some of her grandchildren were there; others were sitting near her bed in chairs. I said "Addassa, I'm here." Addassa was mama's middle name, which I endearingly started using when she first became ill. She opened her eyes for a fraction of a second then quickly closed them. I thought to myself, *"She heard me."* I then laid half my body beside hers. A few minutes later, my daughter came where I was and said she *had* to be beside her.

From upstairs, I could hear our pastor arriving, and talking to the family in the living room. He then made his way up the stairs into mama's room. He greeted mama, and all my heart could focus on was her slight breathing. He then said, "Let's pray." With his hand touching my mother's, he started praying. All I remember him saying in the prayer was, "Lord, send your angels to escort your daughter into the kingdom of heaven," and with those words I felt my mom… my mother…my MAMA taking her last breath. She had gone home to glory. Her pastor, whom she loved dearly, and her grandchildren and children, her family, prayed her into heaven. I immediately began to ask, "God, where is my miracle I've been waiting for? WHERE?"

It was 10:45am, my mother's body was lying on her bed, covered with her prayer shawl. I jumped into my car to make my way to work. Unfortunately, I was still scheduled on my working hours, and my shift started at eleven. But this day was unlike all other days! The woman who has loved me my entire life without reservation had just passed away! "I've got to get out of here," I told myself. I was mad, disappointed, and angry with God. He took my mom from me. I prayed, fasted, and stood fast on His Word. I had worked on my faith because I wanted to please Him (Heb. 11:6). I talked to Him, asked Him, believing that, "If you will, you would show up, and a healing would occur," yet she is gone.

I know my God is the God of miracles, He has always shown up for me whenever I needed Him. HE DID IT THEN! However, where was my mother's miracle I was waiting for?

> "Where were you, God, when I came to You, haven't You heard me? Haven't You cared about me? It wasn't time for mama to go home! No! Not now," I cried to the Lord,

"There was still so much for her to see and enjoy, like seeing her daughters and grandchildren getting married, living to celebrate their accomplishments, and enjoying her great grandchildren. I used Your Word, James 5:14, Philippians 4:19, Mark 5:34, 1 Peter 2:24 and many more, but my favorite verse was Isaiah 53:5. I spoke with the authority you have given me on this earth. I bound and loosened, I decreed and declared, I commanded, I made declarations. I rebuked Satan. I claimed healing in Your name. I didn't put my hope in things or doctors, I trusted You, for You have magnified Your Word above all Your name (Ps. 138:2; KJV). I fixed my eyes upon You, Father. I prayed that mama would find favor with You. I relied on YOU. I believed You would take care of it all. Father, I am struggling now with my emotions; my heart and mind are at war. Faith is saying one thing, and facts are presenting another. No exclamation; my mother just died and I chose to go to work. My heart aches and I'm overwhelmed with fear and sadness. I feel vulnerable and uncertain. I'm downcast and doubt wants to creep in... HELP..."

At work, I sat in silence in the darkness of my room with an empty mind, no Scripture, not a thing. But God didn't leave me like this, for the Bible says that *"The Lord is near to the brokenhearted, and saves the crushed in spirit"* (Ps. 34:18). At that moment, the Spirit of God took me back to one day in mama's room when she was lying in her bed worshiping and praising the Lord. I could hear her saying, "Devil, you think you got me, but know for sure that *for those who love God all things work together for good, for those who are called according to his purpose"* (Rom. 8:28)." I knew some words were missing, but I knew that, at that time, God heard the words of her heart. "I'm going home to heaven to my Savior," she said when she saw me walking into the room, "Paulette, I want to go home."

It was then that God showed me He had released her spirit and granted her the desire of her heart. It was then that I started bawling. It felt like my heart was shattering, and my eyes and mouth were releasing the pressure that was building up from within. Tears were streaming down my face, and right then and there, I released the angry, disappointment, and hurt I had bottled inside. I found myself repenting.

I believe we serve a mighty God who understands our emotions, our sadness, and our pain. He is a God who loves us to the end, and cares about every aspect of our lives. He is always there with me and I stand proudly on that assurance. *"Since then we have a great high priest who has passed through the heavens, Jesus, the Son of God, let us hold fast our confession. For we do not have a high priest who is unable to sympathize with our weaknesses, but one who in every respect has been tempted as we are, yet without sin. Let us then with confidence draw near to the throne of grace, that we may receive mercy and find grace to help in time of need"* (Hebrews 4:14–16).

This is My Prayer:

Father, You promised there would be faith, strength, and hope available for us to contest life's problems. Lord Jesus, I pray that You give me the strength I need when anxiety buries my dreams and when illnesses paralyze my hope. My burdens are heavier than my shoulders can bear. God, You know my secret fears; I offer them to You and ask that You give me mounts of courage as I look to You. You know NO fear. Let Thine will be done and Your kingdom come. In Jesus' name, Amen!

Words of Reflections

WHEN DOVES CRY

Chapter Seven
If Not for God
By: Senator LeAnna Washington

I was born to a promiscuous sixteen years old mother and a thirty years old "street guy" father, who had a taste for fresh young girls. My grandparents faced many problems with mommy. Long before I was born, she would disappear for days. When she came home, she slept, woke up, ate, got dressed and said she was going to the store, returning several days later. And it wasn't long before she got pregnant with me. Mommy was so happy but it was no big deal for my father, for she was one of many young girls who lived in the neighborhood, and who carried his babies. I was born the day after her seventeenth birthday, and she named me after her, LeAnna. The doctor who delivered me said to my mother, "she is as cute as a cookie." And that became my nickname, Cookie.

I was raised by my grandparents for the early years of my life, as my mother persisted in her bad girl attitude. Soon after that, my aunt, who had four children of her own, took over the responsibility of raising me. Mommy was known to show up periodically to claim her daughter. She would hang around for six weeks, and then she was gone again. One day, she came back and said she got an efficiency apartment, and was ready to take her baby.

Our second-floor apartment had a padlock that was used to keep intruders out and me in. I don't remember much as a toddler, but I do remember sleeping on a cot in front of the oven, and the canned Salisbury steak cooked by running hot tap water or the soft-boiled eggs cooked the same way, which were our frequent items and were unforgettable. Child abuse was not a term used during my growing-up years, it was just "getting beaten." There were always bruises, busted lips, black eyes, and everything else in between.

As time went by, I was back with my aunt, for mommy was gone again. Years later, she showed up again and took me to live with her and my new stepfather. It wasn't bad; after all, I had my own room, as well as a dining room, and a living room. Things seemed better, but mommy was very mean, and actually I don't think she could be anything else. The older I became, I found myself behaving just like her, but I dared not stay out past my curfew. I did all my bad stuff in daytime, and, guess what, I got pregnant at sixteen.

Mommy took me to the doctor. She told him I was her daughter. She was thirty and I was only sixteen. The doctor asked too many questions that we walked out of his office extremely angry, and that was the end of my prenatal care. Seven months later, my first child was born, making my mother and me very happy. Mommy, unlike before, was a good grandmother but… she didn't babysit. This meant that the baby had to be with me wherever I go. Still, seven months later, I was pregnant again, and gave birth, nine months later, to another son. I was still abused by mommy, but she didn't do this to her grandsons. The abuse was evident, so I was soon invited to stay with my sons' father's family.

Be careful what you wish for. Living with this man's family was good and bad, for no land is without stones, and no meat is without bones. We were fighting a lot, me and my son's father, with many visible bruises. One day my mom showed up and asked what happened to her daughter's face? He answered, "We are getting married." I was so happy that I forgot about the black eye.

The day after the wedding I had another black eye. So much for love. We moved from my husband's family house into public housing, and it was as if I got out of the frying pan into the fire. We fought like cats and dogs. Every glass, mirror, lamp, and anything else that could break was broken, but after all this was our home. Our children were always afraid because they lived in a warzone with the constant fighting between their parents.

One year later, we were able to buy our own house, IF NOT FOR GOD. But the fighting never stopped. Once again, I was pregnant but now I was married, "I had a husband." Nine months later, we had a beautiful baby girl. Our relationship never changed for the better but only for the worse. My husband began to physically and verbally abuse our children. He could snap his fingers, and point to his construction boots, and my little boys would immediately struggle to take those big boots off. IF NOT FOR GOD, I wouldn't have lasted in this marriage for eight long years.

Because of the issues I was facing in my personal life, and the constant abuse from my mother and my husband, a friend recommended that I should see a therapist. During my therapy sessions, I discussed the long years of abuse from my mother, and later from my husband. After a lot of discussions, my therapist explained to me that my negative feelings toward my mother did not give me the right to punish her for abusing me. She said that my responsibility was to be a good daughter to my mother, and she suggested we invite her in for our last session.

When the day came for the session, mommy showed up looking strange. The therapist spoke with her about the issues I was having regarding my childhood. Mommy was enraged because I had shared these things with someone. The therapist asked my mother if she loves me and her response was no. The therapist asked her, "Why don't you love your daughter?" And her response was, "Every time I love someone I get hurt." Then, mommy asked the therapist, "Are you done yet?" The therapist replied, "Yes;" and my mother got up and walked out the door.

My therapist began discussing the session with me, explaining that mommy's feelings were about getting pregnant and not getting the man she wanted to marry. This could be the reason she disliked me. It took me a while to grasp what she had said. After a lot of thinking, I decided to reach out to my mother, so I went to visit her. IF NOT FOR GOD, who used the therapist to explain to me my role as a daughter, and who helped me to build a mother–daughter relationship, I wouldn't have done any of that. The therapist also encouraged me to return to school. I followed her advice and completed the GED program at Temple University.

I worked hard to build a relationship with my mother, but she rejected her grandchildren as she did with her own child. One of the things I realized from my visits to her was that something was seriously wrong with her. I started taking her to doctor appointments, and there, we were told she suffered some mental health issues. I then recalled when she stabbed my stepfather and went to prison for that. My stepfather did not press charges against her, and eventually she came home and took care of him. The incident was never discussed again, until years later when she threatened to stab her husband, who is now deceased, again. When we went to her next appointment, I told the doctor about that. She said to him, "I will stab him for taking my money." So, he said, "I would like for you to be admitted to the hospital for evaluation," and she said, "Okay." Her threatening to do bodily harm forced him to place her in a psychiatric evaluation unit.

The evaluation and the series of tests revealed that mommy suffered from mental health disorders which were never dealt with. I always thought something was wrong. This explained her behavior throughout the many years. The doctor recommended that I get power of attorney for mommy and I did. She was admitted to a facility, and remained there until the day she died twelve years later. During her stay in the facility, I saw many personalities come and go, but the medications helped to keep her calm. All the time of suffering and all the time we lost by her behavior was due to her mental illness. We became very close during those years that she spent in the nursing home facility, it was as if she was my baby. Despite the hardship, heartache, and pain, and despite all the past, I thank God for enabling me to get to know her and love her. I thank

God for I did not become an abuser for my children, instead, a loving mother, with three children, four adult grandchildren, and four great grandchildren. To God be the glory. *For we know that for those who love God all things work together for good, for those who are called according to his purpose* (Romans 8:28).

Telling my story has led me to many other women who needed to hear about something bad turning good. I've been to prisons, homeless shelters, and drug and alcohol programs, telling my story to anyone who would listen. My life had its ups and downs, twists, and turns, and because of this there were a captive audience relating to my experience. *Blessed be the God and Father of our Lord Jesus Christ, the Father of mercies and God of all comfort, who comforts us in all our affliction, so that we may be able to comfort those who are in any affliction, with the comfort with which we ourselves are comforted by God* (2 Corinthians 1:3-4). Anyone can hurt, but only God can heal, if you just ask Him and believe He will bring you through. Prayer changed many things in my life, enabling me to grow and be stronger.

Every accomplishment in my adult life was always for the sake of my children, for I wanted to be a good role model for them. I also wanted to provide them with a stable environment and structure. I went back to school, and that step changed my life and the lives of my sons and daughter.

You may be an abused child, teenaged parent, high school dropout, or a victim of domestic violence, and still carry that survival kit with you. Every day of your life you can achieve anything. It is never too late. The God of your salvation is always there to make your feet like the deer's, and to make you tread on your high places (Hab. 3:18-19). **But if not for God.**

When asked what my favorite Scripture is, I reply, Psalm 23 which begins with: *"The Lord is my shepherd I shall not want,"* and concludes with *"Surely goodness and mercy shall follow me all the days of my life."* This allows me to say, "But if not for God."

God knows everything about us, He knows the bad and good things in our lives. Thus, prayer will bring you comfort. When you ask God for help, He will give you peace which surpasses all understanding (Phil. 4:7). Know well that God is all-knowing and there is nothing hidden from him, but all are naked and exposed to his eyes, including every secret (Heb. 4:13). Don't give up! Tell Him your problems and invite Him to your current situation. God's favor will set before you an open door, which no one is able to shut, and He may also close a door which no one is able to open (Rev. 3:8).

God promised He would never leave us nor forsake us (Heb. 13:5). Maybe we had times in our lives when we felt alone, but truly we were not. "The Footprints in the Sand" story assures us that God was carrying us during all those times. We have an amazing God. When we feel weak, He'll make us strong. When we are confused, He will give us clarity. When we think we can't, we can declare that we can do all things through Christ who strengthens us (Phil. 4:13).

It doesn't matter how difficult a situation may seem or appear to be, God can and will change anything negative into positive. He did this for me, and surely will do it for you.

My Father in heaven, I thank You for Your favor, and for carrying me when I even thought I didn't need to be carried. God, You know all about my story, and I know that if not for You, I would have been in many other places, but instead, I'm now in Your hands. I thank You for turning my life around and drawing me closer to You. Lord, I ask

You to bless and keep my children, grandchildren and great grandchildren. Lord, bless those who need Your grace and mercy but do not know them yet. In Jesus' name, Amen!

Words of Reflections

WHEN DOVES CRY

Chapter Eight

From Crushed...To Joy! By: Dr. Mary Floyd Palmer

My mother, known to me as "ma, mom, or mommy," was the middle child of five siblings, and the only child who was bold and fearless. She grew up in Richard Allen Homes, and was a fierce fighter if you messed with her family. As a young teenager, she was the caregiver to her blind aunt, and also to an aging aunt, and an uncle. Therefore, her social life was very limited.

After graduating from high school, she was gainfully employed as a Microbiology Technician at the former Medical College of Philadelphia Hospital, better known as Women's Medical Hospital. She shared her salary with her mom (my grandnan) to make ends meet for the household. Seven years later, she met, courted, and married my father.

Now a married and pregnant woman, her plan was taking her maternity leave after delivery, then returning to work. Instead, the day of my birth was her last day at work. She knew that her place was at home, taking care of her husband, her child, and her house. Hearing this always humbled me, because it speaks of the loyal and dedicated housewife, mother, and family member she was.

More important to my mother than her family was her relationship with Jesus Christ. She became a believer at age nineteen, and re-dedicated herself and her life at Billy Graham's Crusade in Philadelphia, in January 1962. Oddly enough, my father was at this same crusade. This was the glue that cemented their relationship, and led to their marriage in August of the same year. My parents were both faithful in service at their home church, and dedicated to working with young people during a turbulent time when gang wars were very prevalent. My mother served as Church Clerk, Deaconess, and Sunday School Teacher at the church where I was born.

When my dad joined the staff of an outreach Christian organization in north Philadelphia, mom was right there as his greatest supporter and co-laborer, while at the same time being a mother of two toddler girls and pregnant with her third child. She was the perfect helper fit for him (Gen. 2:18), and the excellent wife who is far more precious than jewels (Prov. 31:10). She kept the young girls under her wings, but also became "mom" to many of the young men who came at the center asking for refuge.

Finally, the Lord led my parents to relocate to Germantown. There, the weekly Bible clubs were held on our front porch for the neighborhood children. As a licensed minister and a police officer, my dad was among the first who witnessed the results of the "turf wars." He was trying his best as a cop, and even requested to work in specialized units, like juvenile aid, and gang prevention; but it still wasn't enough. This was taking a heavy toll on him, but he knew he needed to do more. So, one day, mom challenged him and said (paraphrasing), "Well, do something about it! You have got to get out into those streets and save those kids' lives by telling them about Jesus, and making them see that this senseless killing must stop." So, my dad began his non-profit organization that was geared to the streets with an "in-your-face-message" that would cause young people to think before they act! Subsequently, he resigned from the police force, and went into full-time ministry.

As a housewife, mom was consistent and tenacious. She believed in setting her house in order, and rarely missed a deadline. Every day, we had breakfast and dinner at home, clean pressed clothes laid for us to wear, and hot lunch at school where she served as a volunteered parent. For her, in order to take care of her children and provide for them, no task was too big or too small. She was the leader of the pack, and she served all week during our entire tenure as students, including high school. Mom drove me and my sisters everywhere we needed to be: church six days a week, school five days a week, music lessons twice a week, choir rehearsal once a week, etc. Truly, this woman looked well to the ways of her household, and did not eat the bread of idleness, therefore, we rose up and called her blessed (cf. Prov. 31:27–28).

Mom was just as formidable with her siblings, always the protector and the "go-to" sister who would fix anything. I remember when my aunt was a crime victim and called my mom, she was right there. She was not any different for her younger brother whom she cared for until he passed. Her happiest moment was when he accepted

Christ as his personal Savior, after forty years of witnessing to him, seeing him being baptized, and becoming a member of her church, and done with smoking and drinking after 50 years. Glory to God!

The first crush occurred in 1973. Mom got pregnant in her tubes and had to go through a surgery. During the medical tests, she was diagnosed with uterine cancer, and had to undergo a complete hysterectomy. At the tender age of 36, this was a real blow, but necessary! My grandnan, who was taking care of my sisters and me, told me what was happening after I heard mommy crying. I went into her room and told her I was sad that she was upset. She hugged me and said, "I will be alright. I have too much work to do. You pray and God will take care of the rest."

On the day of her procedure, I remember giving her a kiss and telling her to "hurry back." As dad drove off, I knew deep inside that mommy was coming back home, and would be okay. It wasn't until a few years later that mom and I talked about that first experience, when I was diagnosed with cancer at age 22.

I was a young married woman, mother of two children, and I was told this "crushing blow" shortly after the birth of my second child, my precious daughter. Mommy shared her experience with me, woman to woman, and the reality of "her crushed spirit"—her inability to have more children. However, she readily admitted that God does all things well, that He doesn't make mistakes. Despite this disappointment, she loved Him the more for the three beautiful girls she was honored to have. She believed from all her heart that every good gift and every perfect gift is from above, coming down from the Father of lights, with whom there is no variation or shadow due to change (Jam. 1:17). She encouraged me to love my children, despite my broken marriage, and to know that *this* [crushing moment] *too, will pass*. She prophesied that I would be different than her, and that God would allow me another chance to have more children. At that time, I saw a different side of mom, and came to appreciate her in a different way. No more was she just mommy, she was my friend.

After my treatment course, I went into remission. After that, I was blessed with a new marriage and two more healthy sons! My second son (third child) was born on mommy's birthday, and was the first grandchild (although number 6) born in the delivery room live before her eyes. As he was coming into the world, she shouted "Hallelujah" over and over again with tears flowing. Moments after he was born, she held him, and thanked me for allowing her the privilege of such personal and precious moment which she would never forget. She belted out singing the chorus of "To God Be The Glory." What a powerful moment! She then made a vow, if God allowed it that she live to see her sixth great-grandchild born live as well. I was sure that was going to happen, **but ...**

The second crush came when mom was diagnosed with aggressive breast cancer in January 2012. Before that, she was so stubborn about going to the doctor for follow-up because of the family history. I got tired of her excuses for not going. So, her best friend, my aunt Margaret, and I, were forced to trick her. We took her to lunch and then I drove her to her doctor's. She fussed, but got the mammogram and we were happy the results were okay. I think it was a sign of relief.

Just about one month later, mom complained of breast pain and felt some lumps. I told her to go get it checked out, but she stubbornly gave me excuses, usually related to the church calendar, but I insisted. After showing me some leakage, I made the appointment, and she went for another mammogram. The results and biopsy confirmed the doctor's doubts: cancer. As we were speaking with the doctor, I had that sense of sadness I felt before, years earlier, but I was confident that mom was going to champion this, and that God was going to heal her. She was a strong stubborn woman, and her fighting spirit would not let her give up. She agreed to have the surgery and a date was set in March.

Later that night, we sat together, talking like two "old hens." She shared with me some very personal experiences about her life she admitted she never shared before, but she wanted me to know that she had overcome some tough things in life, and she wasn't bitter towards God at all. Instead, she was in love with Jesus and she knew she would not have made it without Him. We hugged, prayed together, and went to bed for about one hour. (You do know she was up and getting the day started…smh). I treasured that time because this was one of three most vulnerable moments I had with her. You see, for me, mom was one of the strongest women in her faith, among her family and her Church. She was as steady as a rock, the backbone that stabilized us and others. For my own selfish reasons, I wasn't ready to see that changed. She survived the surgery, recuperated in record time, finished her chemo and radiation treatment, then went into remission. Once finished, she was back in action, running things, just as busy and strong as ever. I was sure that all would turn well, **but**….

The third crush was when her cancer returned and metastasized to her brain. Thankfully, one of my sisters rushed her to the hospital, and they immediately transferred her to Jefferson because of their world-renowned expertise in Neurology. Her care team was led by one of the nation's leading experts, who recommended immediate surgery to remove a mass located at the base of her brain stem. Twenty-four hours later, after mom signed for the procedure, she underwent an aggressive surgery with 30% survival rate. She said to me, "Mary, I am ready to see Jesus. If I didn't make it, you make sure my great grandbabies, especially Kiy and Kay, your dad and sisters will be fine. And the church, well, you know how folks are. No matter what, you better not stop doing ministry, especially winning souls. I love you." I thanked her for everything she ever did for me and my family, and was sure that, **this too shall pass**.

Mikiyah and Mikayla were the twin reasons why my mom fought so hard to get well after her last cancer battle. Because of their fragile birth and high risk of survival, mommy took it upon herself–ahead of me and my daughter–to make sure they had everything they needed. She prepared their daily food, and greeted the transport team that picked them up with a smile, some treats, and of course, some Jesus. She never missed one morning seeing them off, or any medical appointment, and was their passionate and fierce protector. They loved their "YaYa," and, God knows, she also loved and spoiled them. This didn't lessen her love for her grandchildren, but she was most grateful to see the third generation, her great grandchildren. These girls won her heart and I knew their presence was what she needed. My daughter, who was her ace, and I, just "got out the way," and let her do Nana. Mom exhibited the same tenacious care for my daughter after she suffered a traumatic injury at the tender age of one year. My mom then sent me to work and assured me that she would take care of my baby girl. And I trusted her with that. So, to see this happening again with the next generation gave me the greatest comfort. This was "legacy in the making," and I yielded to the wisdom and presence that my children were privileged to have by living with mom. She thanked me many times a day for allowing her the opportunity to pour into them in the early years of their lives.

Then, the final crushing blow came. Mom was dying. We met with the medical team and they informed us that they had done all they could, and now she needed hospice. This seemed so surreal to me. I heard what they said, but believed God. There was a miracle in the making. It was not to be so.

Mom spent her last days at a beautiful home-like hospice facility with excellent staff, and especially mom's assigned nursing assistant. This woman was saved, and she and mom would have "church" together while she took care of mom's hygiene needs. The last day that I heard mommy's voice, she spoke about Jesus, her babies, thanked me for being there, and then said, "I'm tired and ready to see Jesus." I cried and hugged her, and she went into sleep. Four days later, while sitting in her room, mom took her last breath. It was so peaceful. As I looked at her, I imagined the JOY she must have just experienced. I imagined her waving her hands in worship, and looking at Jesus' face! Although I was crushed in my human spirit, I cried, not of sorrow, but of joy for having mommy for 78 years, and of assurance that I will see her again.

May I encourage you with the words of Psalm 34:18, which say: "The Lord is near to the brokenhearted, and saves the crushed in spirit." This is the last thing most of us want to hear during or after crushing moments, but the fact still remains that we have no power to prevent any of our life's experiences, especially the death of a mother. There is no other loss like that. Many never get over it, but instead, allow that loss to keep them bruised or broken. But for those who do have hope, we do not have to grieve or act as if we don't (cf. 1 Thess. 4:13). It is heartbreaking, yes! Painful, yes! Unbelievable, yes! Daunting, indeed! But praise God for Jesus who is my (our) Balm in Gilead (Jer. 8:22). He can and will heal you, stirring up inside you the Holy Spirit's fruit called joy. Remember this truth very well, Psalm 30:5b says, "Weeping may tarry for the night but joy comes with the morning." At the breaking of each new day, the night is gone. When you see this, shout for joy! I am quite sure I will see mommy again, somewhere round the throne! Oh, what unspeakable JOY that will be!

*Words of Reflections*_____

WHEN DOVES CRY

Chapter Nine
Gone Now but Never Forgotten
By: Dr. Joanna Birchett

Sometimes in the mornings, I would be awoken by the sound of my mother, the late Muriel Bernice Robinson Ottey, "Mama Ottey Cash" as she is affectionately known in the entire neighborhood, singing songs like, "Farther along we'll know all about it, farther along we'll understand why," and other Christian songs, while she was preparing some really good Jamaican breakfast for her family. At a young age, I never understood why she would wake up so early, making sure everything was prepared before my dad left for work, and before we would leave for school. I look back today, and I can say that though at that time my mother was not saved, she still carried the qualities of a Proverbs 31 woman, and that this is where all her children got their quality of excellence from. I know I mentioned she was singing; what was amazing is that my mother was not a church goer, yet she would sing praises to God, all the time!

My mom was a strong woman, a woman of steel. And one main thing I learned from her was that I can be anything I want. She taught me NEVER to give up. Even with her not getting the best education, she desired the best for all her children. She was a different mother, a go getter; she did what she had to. And one thing I know is that she made sure we went to the best of the best schools. We had to come home with good grades, for she put that Jamaican parental FEAR in us (LOL!).

I can look back today and smile. Maybe she wasn't perfect, we did not have that million dollars house, but we never felt we were not well off. As a wife and mother, she kept it all together.

For me, she was a great companion and confidant even in the most difficult times. She dedicated her life to caring and providing for her family, both physically and emotionally. The pain I feel by writing this chapter is horrific, but I thank God. A mother's love is irreplaceable, therefore, losing her to death is an incredibly painful experience.

I remember getting pregnant at a young age. I was so afraid to tell her, I knew there was no excuse, justification, or reasoning for what I had done. So, I kept going to school (high school), and acting the part as though everything was ok. Sometimes she would ask me, "Jojo, is it that time for you yet?" I would lie in her face and say, "Oh yea mommy, it came already," knowing I was lying through my teeth. This went on for a while, but one day one of my school friends decided to let the cat out of the bag. OH LORD!!!! She came home with me, sat with my mom, and said, "Mrs. Ottey, I know you are going to be mad, but I have to tell you that Joanna is pregnant." I was numb, it felt like my whole world instantly fell apart. I knew I was done, better yet, DEAD!

But lo and behold, to my surprise, my mom turned to me with a stare that shook my ground, and said, "You're pregnant?" I wasn't sure whether I was to answer or run, but I nodded my head. She thanked my friend for letting her know. After my friend left, I assumed that was it, but the mother side in her arose, and she turned to me and said, "This is now your responsibility, you made your bed, now you have to lie down in it." I was shocked; even though the situation was not as sweet as it sounds here, but at least I was still alive. When I think now of my mom, I am able to see how much she loved us. She wasn't perfect, but for me she was. After all that was said and done, she NEVER believed in abortion. And when I recall that time, I can stand today and affirm that she knew I was pregnant. She chastised me very sternly (which was expected), but she NEVER condemned me. I love you, mom, so much, and writing this chapter is bitter sweet for me.

Birth and death have some similarities, they both are monumental occurrences that change your life forever. In many days like today, I get emotional, just hoping that I would have the opportunity to see her or even hear her voice saying, "Jojo, why haven't you called today?"

In stories like mine, people usually jump to the lessons learned from losses or tragedies, that you should live every day to its fullest, or as if it's your last, that you should always say what you think and feel to people you love; tomorrow is not promised, so let the truth be told, for you never know if you'll have another chance.

As the CEO and editor of my own magazine, three years ago, I wrote an article about my mom on Mothers' day, and as I look back now, it was right before she passed. Let me share it with you.

Celebrate your Mom
Article by: Pastor Joanna Birchett

There is nothing in the world like a mother's love. There is so much I can say to my mom, Muriel Bernice Ottey, I want to take a minute to honor her in this article.

My mom lives in the beautiful and sunny island of Jamaica, she was not as educated as some of the other mothers, but I can truly say she instilled good moral ethics in us. She was a dedicated woman, and I have learned so much from her. There were times when I believed I failed her, but she never gave up on me, and that gave me so much motivation to keep pressing on.

I remember getting pregnant at a very young age. And I am so glad that even though my mother was not saved then, she never allowed me to commit myself to abortion. She chastised me really hard, but I see now that it was all worth it.

"Mommy, let me tell you I love you for who you are. No matter what we had to endure, the love I have for you is unexplainable. I thank you for always being there for me. You were my greatest cheerleader. You covered me, took care of me, looked out for me, and I can never repay you for anything you have done. So, I publicly want to tell you: 'I love you.' May the Lord continue to keep you in perfect peace as you keep your mind on Him.

COMPILED BY NEPHETINA L. SERRANO

Published in the Gospel 4 U Magazine

May 2014

Every time I read this article, it brings tears to my eyes. I miss you so much, mom. I cannot put into words the pain I feel when I think about you.

Reality Kicks In

In this life, we have to show love while we still can. Tell someone today that you care, because God has a different plan for tomorrow. I can truly relate to the fact that we should love each other daily, as tomorrow is NOT promised.

About two years ago, I got a call from Jamaica telling me my mom was not doing so well. She had been sick for a while, and her struggle was real. She lost so much weight, and even with all the medicines she was taking, nothing seemed to work. This reminded me of the story of the woman with the issue of blood in the Bible, who tried everything and nothing seemed to work, though she had spent all her living on physicians (Luke 8:43–48). My mother also had an issue of blood that only God could heal, if that was His will for her life.

So, I received the call, and yes, I am a woman of God, but fear gripped me for a minute. "God! Please, this is my mom!" That was all I could think of. My spirit got quiet, my mouth muted, but deep in my spirit I began to pray with great expectancy, reminding God of His Word, *"You keep him in perfect peace whose mind is stayed on you, because he trusts in you"* (Isa. 26:3).

But a strange thing happened; my son called from Jamaica, saying that my mom wasn't responding to anyone. She had lost her speech ability, and the only time she would flinch was when the pain hit her. She refused to go to the hospital, as she knew she was leaving us and she wanted to stay home in the comfort of her own house.

I didn't know whether to fly out immediately to Jamaica, or to stay. My sister, who is a nurse, said we should wait because she could pass while we are on our way to there. So, I continued speaking to the Lord. And in my spirit, the Lord directed me to call and talk to her, so I picked up the phone and asked them to hold it near to her ear, and I said, "Mommy, I know you are in pain, but if you can hear me just moan." Nothing happened. Suddenly, the Spirit of God told me, "pray with her," I began to intercede for my mom with tears rolling down my face, and I asked her, "Mommy, do you believe that Jesus is Lord?" IMMEDIATELY there was a moan!!!! I knew that was God. He wanted to assure me that she was ok spiritually. And right there, I was reminded that 15 years ago my mom came to the United States, and accepted Jesus Christ as her Lord and Savior at my former church (True United), and she got baptized by my Bishop. Her moan, then, was an assurance that she was at peace with God.

It felt as though my mother was waiting for my call, for after we got off that call, and after 48 hours of pain and turmoil, my mom passed away within the hour. She traveled into the hands of Jesus, and I am now at peace within my heart that she is in a better place, no more pain, no more sorrow, no more medications (cf. Rev. 21:4).

Our lives will never be the same without our mom, but I can truly say that I have learned so much from this tragic ordeal. Life for my family will never be the same again, but after all my mom had to endure, after all the pain she had to bear, I am now at peace knowing that she is now in a better place. I am not grieving as others do who have no hope (1 Thess. 4:13).

When I began writing this chapter, I thought to myself, as mad as I felt, I could not be mad. It's funny that I was asked to share my story. I say this because after taking a minute to share these pages, I can feel a peace in my heart. Now I understand the Scripture in Philippians 4:7 *"And the peace of God, which surpasses all understanding, will guard your hearts and your minds in Christ Jesus."* God will give you HIS peace whether in life or death, and the peace is so anointed to heal you from every hurt or pain.

This experience was a therapy for me, and I thank God for these times of reflection, because they allowed me to see that even though my mother is gone, she will NEVER be forgotten, she lives in the great memories that the Lord had allowed me to have, and for this I am thankful.

This song came into my spirit, "Then sings my soul, My Savior God, to Thee, How great Thou art, How great Thou art." God is such an amazing Father, and as I sing this song I am reminded that Muriel Bernice Ottey passed away, but her legacy lives on, and that is why my heart sings today. I am one of the many legacies she left behind, and with the power of the Holy Spirit, I promise to make her proud of me through all my life.

The passing of my mom did something to me, I remember I cried, and then got silent for a while. Maybe I was mad, but never expressed it. I kept it all inside, and my heart spoke to the Lord. I remember thinking to myself, "Why Lord?" And during these times of hurt and pain, He began to reveal to me some deep things; I began to understand that His plans are not mine (cf. Isa. 55:8–9), and the most important thing is that He makes NO mistakes. My mother's passing was not a mistake.

I began to realize that her death brought our family closer, but I must say also that I am able to see a significant change in me as a person. So, I must believe that her death was not in vain, it taught me to love and appreciate EVERYONE, to have compassion, and above all, it taught me that tomorrow is NOT promised to ANYONE. So, while we still have time, we have to love each other, appreciate EVERYONE in our life, as they are all temporary, and I say temporary because we all have an expiration date in this life.

My mother's death made me a much better and stronger person. And while I would much rather have her here with me even just for one more minute, and would trade all these growth moments for that, there's still some value in what I've learned, and I pray that as I share my story in *When Doves Cry,* that would be helping someone else reading it.

The core principle with which I live my life now will sound, at face value, like one of the platitudes I just eschewed above, but we as people can learn from every mistake, or even disappointment. And I thank God for teaching me how to handle this. I have no regrets with my mom's passing, because I know that she loved me and I loved her so much more. She raised up great children and I have to say that God used her to plant good seeds in my life. My mom made sure I go to church even though she did not attend with me. I look back today and see that she was sowing seeds and that was where it begins, *"Train up a child in the way he should go; even when he is old he will not depart from it"* (Prov. 22:6). I get it, mom! Thank you.

Lord I humbly say thank you for giving me the strength to express in words the love and great memories of my mother, bless every reader of this book and grant them your peace, thank you for the years you gave us together and I know I will see her again, one day in Glory, you are a good God and Father and your peace is upon us. I seal this prayer in Jesus name, Amen!

Words of Reflections

WHEN DOVES CRY

Chapter Ten

Though Forsaken... Received by the Lord

By: Corrie Lingenfelter

I remember the day as if it was yesterday. October 29, 2003 at 4:15pm was when I lost my mother. I was only twelve. My mother was diagnosed with stage 3 ovarian cancer when I was 3 years old. The doctors told her she would only live for 3 to 6 months, but God had the final say and gave her almost 10 more years.

My mother was better on the days she wasn't doing chemo or radiation. For her, those days seemed to be the worst. She would come home very tired and fragile, and would sleep the day away into the next. I didn't fully grasp what was going on because one thing my mother didn't do, she didn't give in to her sickness. She taught me the true meaning of strength. She taught me that no matter what I go through, I serve a God bigger than anything! And through Him, who strengthens me, I can do all things (Phil. 4:13).

During the 12 years my mother was still here, she grew to be my best friend. I could tell her anything without being afraid of what she might say or make me feel. She taught me unconditional love. See, I'm adopted. I never really found out until people at school began to ask me why I was different in color than the rest of my family. My family was Caucasian and I was biracial, but my mother never emphasized color to us, so for all, I knew I wasn't different.

I remember coming home that day, crying and asking, "why didn't you tell me you weren't my real mother?!" The tears rolled down her face, but then she smiled that radiant smile and said, "I am your mother." And she explained to me what a mother really is, and told me the story of my biological mother and my adoption, and how God showed me to her even before she met or chose me. See, when we have children we don't get to choose, we are given what God wants us to have. But the fact is that my mother chose to take on raising a child that would be different. She chose to love me before knowing if I would love her back or not. She said "yes" to not only God's will for her life, but for my life as well.

That is why, to this day, I never refer to my parents as foster or adopting parents. They are my parents, my divine gift. That is why I love my name so much. My mother named me Corrie after a famous missionary, Corrie Ten Boom. In the days when the Nazi concentration camps were going on, Ten Boom's family was one of the families that hid Jews. The significance of her story lies in that after being caught, imprisoned, and after her family was taken captive in the concentration camps, and even being tortured and killed in front of her, Corrie still went on to serve God, and she even had to nurse the Nazi's. I always wondered why my mother would give me such a phenomenal namesake. I no longer question that as I now understand who I am in God, now my soul knows very well that I am fearfully and wonderfully made for a purpose (Ps. 139:14; Eph. 2:10).

I learned a lot in such a short amount of time I spent with my mother. She was the exact definition of a Proverbs 31 woman, and I thank God daily for He did see fit to have her find me and raise me into the woman I am today. I wish I could say it has been easy and my life has been amazing since then, but I think the hardest part about losing my mother was when I realized she's been dead longer than she was able to be my mother. I remember well that year, and I remember not getting why I had to be deal with these cards. Wondering if anyone else could relate with having a mother dead longer than she was a mother. Just the thought of it made me sick inside. I started questioning God on why. I also thought back to my biological mother. It was as if I had a double loss, as if I was grieving two mothers.

That was the darkest time in my entire life, and I couldn't even tell anyone about it. I felt I had to be strong for the sake of people around me, for they may think less of me if I showed my weakness. I remember just feeling like I was at a museum. As a pastor's daughter, we have to be polished and in place, showing no weakness to those waiting to see us fail.

I remember the day when everything came full circle. This was when one of my best friends at the time lost her mother almost the same way I lost mine. See, no one was able to comfort her like I was, because I was the only one in our circle who had lost a mother. I remember ministering to her and empathizing with her, and being really able to grieve with her. That day I understood that God allows things sometimes in our lives not because we did anything wrong, but because someone else is waiting for us to help them conquer the same thing we had to overcome.

See, a loss of anything or anyone can be pure hell at the time, but I came to encourage someone that joy does come in the morning (Ps. 30:5)! You may be reading this, crying, and thinking no one understands, but I know someone who does, who in all our afflictions He was afflicted (Isa. 63:9), and His name is Jesus. He will stick to you closer than a brother (Prov. 18:24). See, I have a lot of favorite Scriptures, but the one I want to leave with you today is found in Psalms 27:10 and it reads: *"For my father and my mother have forsaken me, but the Lord will take me in."* Although my mother and my biological mother never left me negatively, I always felt abandoned by them, but I had to mature and realize that even if I felt abandoned, I was never alone, because the day I stopped feeling my mother's embrace, I was able to start feeling my Savior's embrace.

I just want to take some time to tell you how much God loves you. Maybe you are reading this and you've recently lost your mother or maybe it's been years. Maybe you're even reading this and have never lost a mother but someone who has been a mother figure in your life. Whatever the loss is, it has affected you in some way. I want to tell you three things. 1) It is ok to be sad and even cry; however, don't let the enemy keep you there. 2) Cast it on God, for the Bible says in 1 Peter 5:7, *"Casting all your anxieties on him, because he cares for you."* 3) Although some may not understand what you're going through, let them comfort you. The biggest mistake I have made at times is not knowing when to let people help me carry the burden of loss. God will put people in our lives for such a time as this situation, and it's up to us to embrace this.

    I leave you now with this: No matter what things look like, now or in the past, YOUR LATTER WILL BE GREATER (cf. Job 8:7)! It's during the times of mourning and grieving that we tend to be stuck where we are. I charge you to shake it off, let God, the God of all grace, restore you (1 Peter 5:10), and renew your mind, and GO FORTH! This is just a stepping-stone for the next phase and season in your life. Although you might not fully understand now, but it's ok not to have all the answers, for if we had them all, we would no longer need GOD! Let GOD have His way in your life because I am a living example of His goodness even through the sorrows of life!

Remember my beloved to STAY ENCOURAGED!

Lastly, I want to pray with you. Although I am not here in the body, as I write this and pray, I am here with you.

Lord, I humbly come to You, Father, bowing before Your throne. I ask You to clear my heart of anything that hinders my ability to fully experience You and what You have for me. I ask that You comfort me and comfort the person reading this right now, for You are the God of all comfort (2 Cor. 1:3)! Search us, O Lord, and clean up anything that still needs to be cleaned up, and lead us in the way everlasting. Give us peace, O Lord, for today! May we not lean on our own understandings, but in all our ways acknowledge You! Lord, I thank You for the trials because You said in Your Word to *"count it all joy when we meet trials because we know this is just a testing of our faith, and that in the end we will come out perfect and complete, lacking in nothing"* (Jam. 1:2-4)! Lord, we honor You and we call on Jehovah Shalom, the God of peace, to comfort us through this time of loss and mourning. Lord, stick closer to us than a brother in this time. Lord, we thank You despite what it feels like, we say thank You! Lord, thank You for Your love that covers everything we've gone through.

Lord, we ask all this in Your Son's name, in Jesus' name. Amen.

Words of Reflections

WHEN DOVES CRY

Chapter Eleven

The Virtuous Mother

By: Deidra Roussaw

Carrie Mae Camp was a one of a kind mother of eleven children. She was known in our community, as well as throughout and outside the city of Philadelphia as Mantua's favorite mom. My mom was born in Franklin, VA. She grew up with her parents and siblings. She was the type of mom everyone wanted. When I was younger I just couldn't understand why people were so attached to her. I always thought, "Why couldn't they be excited about their own moms?" I guess I may have been a little jealous and selfish because this person was actually the only person whom I could always count on no matter what the situation was.

I have very fond memories of my mom, my hero!

She worked very diligently to provide for her children. Every morning, she was up at the crack of dawn, tending to housework, cooking, laundry, preparing our clothes, and overseeing us perform our daily chores.

Sunday was my mom's only day off. Before we went to church every Sunday, we would assist her with laundry, and we would get ready for shopping immediately after church. My oldest brother, Darryl, always used to meet us after church, taking us to 9th and Washington Streets, to the place that was known by the Italian Market. We would then go to a certain sandwich shop to get roast pork sandwiches. My mom's favorite store was Cannuli Bros, which was a family owned establishment. We were mesmerized to see the butcher cut up a whole pig and cow. We spent there at least two hours waiting for them to cut, grind, and season our meats; in the meanwhile, we were allowed to drink unlimited hot cocoa and tea especially at winter because back then it was bitter cold.

Once we finished all the food shopping, we would go to the children's clothing store at 4th and South Street, where my mom would buy for my little sisters and me, as well as for my nieces, some fashionable clothes. Whenever my other nephews and nieces would come over, they were guaranteed new outfits too. It was always at least four to six of us, and my mom would pick out the outfits and have us try on EVERYTHING one at a time. This was so boring to us because it took so long, but afterwards we would be excited because every Sunday we knew we were getting something new. Whoever came with us would get whatever we received; my mom was such a fair person.

After she took care of the children, my mom would step next to Breacher's Dress Shop, where she would buy her fashionable clothes. Afterwards, we would go around the corner to Jim's Steaks to get cheese steaks. This was almost every Sunday's regiment and we loved it.

When we got back home, our work was cut out for us. We lived in a large three-story house, which was very plush. Growing up, I only remember living in one house. The boys shared the third floor and the girls the second. The boys did all the heavy chores, such as carrying food, taking out the trash, keeping the yard clean, shoveling the snow, and so on. We, the girls, were responsible for assisting our mother with the laundry and with cooking the food.

Since there were so many of us, my mom used to cook a huge Sunday's dinner every Sunday, which consisted of at least but not limited to 3 meats, 3 starches, and 3 vegetables. Everything was made fresh; we, the girls, learned to peel potatoes before we were around seven. At the age of eleven, we were able to cook four-course meals. My mom always purchased cases of fresh fruit, and she never cooked anything processed, always fresh. And since my mom worked at least six days of the week, she always made sure we had enough to eat. We had a deep freezer in the basement, which was always full. On Mondays, my friends would come over my house after school to get some home-cooked food which I took for granted because sometimes I just wanted junk food like steaks, hoagies, pizza, etc.

We grew up in a very strict environment, my mom didn't play any games with us and never spared the rod (cf. Prov. 13:24). We were a fighting family; we didn't start fights, but my mom always told us that if we were to get into a fight, we had better kick butt, or she would kick ours.

Although my mom worked six days a week, I had nine other siblings looking over my shoulder. My older siblings carried out mom's instructions; there was no getting around it, my mom said, and it is settled.

Every holiday, including St. Patrick's Day, Memorial Day, July 4th, and Labor Day, my mom would buy new outfits for the younger children. We would all have red, white, and blue short sets or dresses. For Easter, we would get a church outfit, and an Easter Monday outfit to wear back to school. For Thanksgiving, dinner would start as soon as my mom arrived home from work, and we would be up all night, cooking and listening to Christmas music.

Christmas in our household was tremendous; my older siblings had their own professions and/or married. We loved this holiday as this was the day when everyone can meet together to celebrate and get some really good gifts. After we attended midnight mass, we would start preparations for our huge family's celebration.

My mom always made sure we had everything for Christmas; we always received new coat and new clothes on top of everything else. If you said you believe in Santa Claus, you would receive a bunch, but the moment you confess there was no Santa Claus, you receive less. That is why I believed in Santa Claus until I was sweet sixteen.

On Christmas morning, we would get up around 5:00am. We always had the biggest tree, and there would be piles and piles of presents. Once we all received our new toys, we would play for the entire morning (this was a treat because my mom didn't tolerate a bunch of playing). In the afternoon, we would take our baths and wait for the older siblings to come over. My mom ran a tight ship in our house; every time the doorbell rang we would have to yell out who was at the door. I thought this was so embarrassing, but once I reached adulthood, I certainly understood.

My older brothers, Darryl, Russell, Gary, Reggie, Bobby, and Michael, were always the best brothers ever; they are all some of the kindest men I've ever known. However, my older sisters, Flo, Pam, and Pearl, were my heartbeats, they took really good care of my little sister Nicole and me. When Catina, Fatima, Nikesha, and William came along they were like my little fan club. Since we weren't allowed to go outside, we would create our own fun such as talent shows, fashion shows, dance contests, and so on. Whenever my mom purchased a bushel of crab, we would create our own crab feasts. And when my mom did allow me to go outside, I had to take my nieces and nephews with me, which was fine because they were fun for the most part, and it kept me out of trouble because one of my nieces would tell everything. My mom didn't start any trouble but she was very feisty.

These are my childhood memories, and I truly appreciate my mom for covering and taking care of all her children and grandchildren. Seeing my mom doing the things she did, I was able to follow suit. Children normally do what you do, not what you say. But when it came to my mom, we ALL did what she said and did. We were reared with respect for our elders; when we saw an adult, we were taught to speak first even if they were across the street.

I could go on and on speaking about my mom, as she was a fashionable stylist and so were her children. She always made sure we had all our needs. She didn't borrow or lend money, she was a well-rounded person, always at someone's rescue. Although we were a large family, my mom made space for my cousins if needed. There was nothing fake about this woman, if she liked you, you will surely know it, if she didn't like you she would keep her distance.

When I had my own daughter, there was no other name I thought would fit but Carrie, she became "Little Carrie." My mom was named after her grandmother and now my only daughter was named after her grandmother, and these two had a beautiful bond. My mom was always my number one supporter.

One of my fondest memories was when my dad passed away; my mom had more than enough on her policy to funeralize and bury him. However, a few days after his death, and with the remainder of the policy, she took all of us shopping, she wanted to lessen our pain. She always made sure her children came before herself, and for this we've always adored her beyond measure.

For all of this, my siblings and I know that we had a mom that was blessed beyond measure. According to the Bible, my mom was that virtuous woman (Prov. 31:10; KJV). Proverbs 31:28 says, *"Her children rise up and call her blessed!"*

On Thanksgiving Day, November 27, 2014, I received a phone call telling me my mom was in excruciating pain and didn't want to go to the hospital. My heart was so heavy I couldn't understand. I was so dysfunctional that my daughter had to help me getting dressed, getting my car out of the garage, and she drove me to my mom's house. I couldn't function because what my daughter didn't know was that the Lord spoke a word to me that He was preparing me because He was taking my mom home to be with Him.

I've had some major encounters with the Holy Spirit, but when it comes to my momma I couldn't understand a thing. I kept asking the Lord if He really wanted to hurt my siblings and me that bad. We'd already lost two brothers, and now He wanted to take my mom. I couldn't share this with anyone not even my husband. I began to get into my quiet space, because if the Lord was taking our matriarch, I really needed Him to speak life into that very dull situation. I cried in the shower every morning prior to mom's leaving her earthly body. I had very few words for everyone; the reality of my mom going to be with the Lord wasn't resonating with my soul.

On that day, December 17, 2014 at 5:00am, one of my older brothers called me saying, "The doctor needed to meet with the family." I knew that would be the last day I would see my mom in the flesh. The day prior she kept waving her hand, I knew she was bidding us, her children, grandchildren, and great grandchildren a farewell, as she was being ushered into the presence of the Lord.

This was the worst bittersweet moment for me because we live as Christians, which means we have to be Christ-like, yet the flesh always kicks in in these situations; I wanted my mom here with me and my siblings. I didn't want to witness her taking her last breath. And as my family is so huge that I wasn't able to have any quiet time with the Lord; I found a quiet room to pray and hear from Him. Once I received a text from my daughter, I knew it happened, I knew the Lord had granted me my forever ANGEL!

Since I had a bunch of siblings, we knew what our mom wanted, she always informed us on what to do. My mom had more than enough for us to bury her, and everyone had a task. My task was choosing her casket, and since my mom was so sharp, I knew this had to be done right.

My mom went home to be with the Lord during the Christmas holiday, it was a sad year for my family. But during that time, the Lord sent me twelve women who called to express their condolences and to inform me that everything would get better. This was a blessing because God knew exactly what I needed, even before I ask (Matt. 6:8). Because all these women had lost their moms prior to me losing mine, they were able to comfort me. Moreover, all my friends and church family were very supportive, I just thank God for this amazing support system.

The day came when my siblings and I would lay our mom, our fabulous matriarch, to rest. I had to come to grips that there will be no more 6:00am phone calls from my mom. When we arrived at the church, there were people all around. My mom was born and died a Roman Catholic. The church was huge, yet it still wasn't enough room, some people were standing, and some were up front with the priest. This spoke volumes about who my mom was as a person.

When my mom's casket was being lowered into the

ground it was a sigh of relief. Since this was around the holidays and my aunt passed away one week prior to my mom, the grief period extended for ten days. These were the ten worst days of my life, yet I was reminded of the Scripture in 2 Corinthians 5:8 which says, *"We would rather be away from the body and at home with the Lord!"*

At that point, I was still sad but it was a different kind of sadness, because I was also rejoicing with the Lord. I knew that God loves me and would not withhold any good thing from me (Ps. 84:11). He also gives us seventy good years, but my mom had additional fifteen. Therefore, I started rejoicing because my mom will always be with me in spirit. One thing for sure is that when my mom went to glory, she was released from her pain, she became free. And I'm now free because my mom is free!

I'm still serving the Lord just as I was raised, knowing I'll see my mom again. It took me some time, but when Jesus left, He said He was leaving us a Comforter, who is the Holy Spirit. I had to allow the Holy Spirit to direct me through my healing process, instead of asking questions such as: "Why did my mom pass away?", and being upset with God. My only question is: "When will my broken heart be healed? When will I be made whole? When will I get to that place where I can think of my mom and smile, instead of crying?" This is a process and it has now been a little over two years. Every time I think of my mom a smile appears. People sometimes ask me why I just smile for no reason, all I can tell them is that my ultimate angel is still watching over me.

If I could leave you with a word of encouragement, it would be to allow the Holy Spirit to minister to you. The process will not be easy but it's worth it. Losing my mom was an ordeal, but God gave me a new deal, not only do I have the Holy Spirit, but I now also have my ultimate angel, who is my mom. And I thank God for loving me at such a time as this. I decree and declare that this too shall happen with you, and that God will restore your joy. I'm a witness because He restored mine.

Father God, once again I come to You asking that You watch over us, Your children, and show us who You are whenever we're hurting or doubting in order to process losing our mom. You promised that You will never forsake us (Heb. 13:5), and we know that You do all things well! I ask You to rock us in Your cradle of love, peace, and grace. Please have mercy on us as we go through this healing process. *We love You because You first loved us* (1 John 4:19). Please allow us to always keep our memories of our mothers close to our hearts. Let us not look to the left nor to the right for help, but let us lift our eyes up to the hills. We believe You are the author and finisher of our faith (Heb. 12:2), keep us on unmovable ground as our feelings may waver from day to day. Some days we don't even know whether we're coming or going, but we trust that if we keep our mind stayed on You, You will keep us in perfect peace (Isa. 26:3). We know that yesterday is gone forever and tomorrow is not promised, all we have is today, which is a marvelous gift from You.

Father God, we know You are a father to the fatherless and a mother to the motherless (cf. Ps. 68:5). We offer up our grief to You because we know you can do all things but fail. Father God, I ask that You take this prayer, shape it, mold it, and make it into what You would have it to be. Encamp Your angels around all who have lost their mothers; guide, guard, and direct us. If we've thought, said, or did anything that wasn't pleasing in Your sight, we ask for forgiveness. Please, let us remember that Your word says, *"Weeping may tarry for the night, but joy comes with the morning!"* (Ps. 30:5). In the matchless, marvelous name of Jesus, who is the CHRIST, we say amen, amen, and amen!

Words of Reflections

WHEN DOVES CRY

Chapter Twelve

Pain of Promise

By: Emma Jean Brant

It was early one Saturday morning my husband I was lying in bed not quite awake
when our telephone rang, still sleepy eyed my husband answered the phone only to get the news that momma as we so endearingly referred had died. My husband was calm yet reluctantly as he hung up the phone began to break down saying, Jean that was the hospital, while clinching me tightly he said your mom is gone. I couldn't do anything but cry out calling her name saying No! No! No! Not my

momma. Honestly, we knew momma was very sick and the possibility of her leaving us was great. However, we did not expect it to be so soon at least not that soon. **(Romans: 8:28)** *"And we know that all things work together for good to them that love God to them who are the call according to HIS PURPOSE"*. It was truly an extremely difficult time but we made it through the rain and the storm.

It was 1958 that my parents moved our family to the city of Philadelphia, which consisted at the time of two girls and one boy. Later born to the union of Robert and Emma Montgomery was the addition of one girl and two more boys.

My father was a free-spirited husband who did exactly what he wanted whenever he wanted. Yet my mother devoted, yielding, and committed as she was allowed and accepted his behaviors no matter how he decided he wanted to be or whatever he wanted to do.

As I can recall this kind of activity went on for many years perhaps 27, until it became the norm for our family. During this time as we were growing up my mother being the nurturer and the committed wife, she remained faithful, loyal, pure and honest to her marriage vows. She honored our dad always as her husband even in his wrong and through her pain. As I remember, I never once heard my mother speak ill of my father despite his unfaithful behaviors and disloyalties to her. She would always defend him no matter what the situation whenever it became necessary. Regardless to how wrong my dad was in actions or behaviors toward her, momma insisted we as the children would honor and respect our daddy. Her exact words would be, "No matter what you see or think of your daddy you are to always respect him" because the bible declares in *(Exodus: 20:12) "Honor your father and thy mother that thy days will be long upon the land which the Lord thy God giveth thee"*, then to make herself clear she would ask, "do you hear me." We would reply, "Yes ma'am momma".

Momma was born June 21, 1933 and died December 30, 1982. Her grandmother Bertha Shealy (whom we referred to so affectionately as Granny) raised her in Goldsboro N.C. due to her and her siblings losing both of their parents by the time she reached the age of eight years old. Despite their significant loss they were raised with strong principles and sound morals, ethics and values that set particular standards in their lives that would hold until their dying day. "This is the crucial factor that you will see has played a significant role in the story I've chosen to share with you".

As we know, while momma and her siblings were raised by their grandmother as primary youth they all shared later in life a commonality of what I have referred to as, *Death by Destruction.*

As a practicing therapist I am one to tell you that when there is a trauma in a family such as the one that had occurred when my mother was a child, and the children are young in age unable to comprehend or come to an understanding of how or why this has happened or how to handle the impact of family tragedies, then we will find that the symptoms of a Mental Health disorder surfaces without appropriate necessary intervention. Now in this case perhaps PTSD, Post Traumatic Stress Disorder played a significant factor of why there were lasting affects due to buried and unattended issues that needed to be addressed to help with the coping mechanisms of losing a loved one especially at such a young age. Of course, PTSD can also cause depression and anxiety which if goes unaddressed can resurface later to impact lives significantly in a negative way. Additionally, when there has not been appropriate intervention to assist family members in the light of traumatic experiences concerning, grief and loss there is inevitably going to be negative repercussions that can and will last a lifetime often causing more grief, pain, depression and anxieties. I truly believe this was the case of my mother and her three siblings. Understand this, just prior to when momma passed away she had become lonely, depressed and had become an Alcoholic. I believe before her transition momma definitely made her Peace with God and He forgave her."

"For Christ also hath once suffered sins the just for the unjust that He might bring us to God, being put to death in the flesh, but quickened by the Spirit". (I Peter 3:18)

But the fact remains my mother, Emma her two sisters and her brother all passed this life and went on to glory. It is my belief that prior to leaving they were all suffering from PTSD and depression and were Alcoholics. I personally believe it was a direct result of all them never receiving any appropriate intervention for their PTSD, Depression, Grief and Loss. Here is my theory. The *Drinking Problem* assessment process is usually three stages: The clustering of specific cognitive, behavioral and psychological elements related to a common process. The interdependences of dependence elements from the negative consequences of substance use.

Now although this theory would identify the beginning of troubles there is a conscience belief there were many other factors within the lives of each individual sibling that directly affected their reasons and decisions to find solace in the alcohol dependence. Although it appeared it was initially just to numb the pain, it quickly became more than a desire but in fact a need. I'm not familiar enough with my mother's sibling to tell their story but I can share my mom's.

*"A **Wounded** Heart"*

Having been present to see my mom go through here is what I know concerning my momma Emma Lee Jones-Montgomery and her progressing dependence on alcohol use.

I grew up in a two parent household and very closely connected and intertwined family that based their home and our up bringing on African American southern principles. Despite being culturally raised in the city of Philadelphia, our family never lost its standards values and typical ways for doing things together. For example, when dinner was served everyone would sit down at the dinner table all together.

In 1958 my parents started their life in the city of Philadelphia when I was five years old those were the happy times of our lives my siblings and me growing, bonding,

developing, and shaping together. Of course we visited our

roots every summer for the first five to seven years until I was about nine or ten years old. Later the visits became less and less frequent as the years passed. During the moments at the dinner table we would hold conversations that connected the dots of communication concerning each of our school day, what was learned or what happened on the way to or from school and things alike that's how involved our parents were in our lives. I remember us being intimately close as a family. While watching my mom and dad show their love for one another as well as their children were a delight but, experiencing their discipline was not so delightful but, it was needed. Our standards, values and typical ways of doing things exhibited a culturally rooted system of the Traditional Southern family. Suddenly it seemed almost overnight that things began to change and fall apart with the family, while it used to be mom and dad home with us now it has been reduced to just mom being home with us and alone most of the time. I remember my mom giving birth to my youngest brother and right after that dad's presence in the home had been reduced to even less frequency. During this time my mom met a woman who had claimed to be her friend instead offered a form of betrayal towards momma in one of the worst ways that a human being could towards another. *("Psalms 118:8-9 "It is better to trust in the Lord than to put confidence in man. It is better to trust in the Lord than to put confidence in princes".* Then it became noticeable that my mom had begun to rely heavily on alcohol. My siblings and I had never witnessed this before but the more frequent my dad stayed out the more my mom became closer and closer acquainted with alcohol until it became her best friend. Listen *(Psa.64: 5)* says, *"We have to encourage ourselves" when things look so bad on the outside". "Trust the Lord with all of your heart and Lean Not to your own understanding". (Prov. 3:5).*

There was a time when my mother would not touch a drink when we were little children not even a beer but now she was drinking strong alcohol in the morning, noon and night. She many times preferred alcohol than eating a meal. Being the second to the oldest, I felt so helpless that I couldn't do anything to help my mom shake that feeling of loneliness, rejection, and betrayal that ultimately became depression. I thought if she could just share what she was feeling with someone else perhaps she would find a different avenue to travel instead of the long, dark lonely one. Mom often times would drink so much she would cry calling out to her own mother who was deceased repeatedly. My siblings and I felt helpless, all we could do was sit and cry with her. Unfortunately, that type of lifestyle for my mother claimed her life in just a few short months. Professionally, my career lead me to social worker. Through this field, I started to gain healing in some of my own life's experiences as I learned to supervise and manage families outside of their home while witnessing the dynamics and circumstances within the home. I began to see more clearly, I truly understand what single mothers go through to raise their families alone since I have lived it through some of my own personal experiences. So many grandmothers are left raising their grand children because mom, dad or both are addicted to substances. I realize somehow with what I was doing and learning as a social worker I wanted to make a bigger difference in the lives of suffering, struggling families.

Father God In the name of Jesus I come to you as humbled as I know how. Lord let someone who reads this story be empowered to know they do not have to stand alone and you are always with us and all we need to do is call upon you. You promised you would answer Prayer. Lord there are so many dying today leaving themselves in the very state the enemy thought he was going to leave my mom in but GRACE be unto God our Father who giveth us the Victory through Jesus Christ our Lord. My FAITH says

MY Mom Made IT IN because she knew and accepted JESUS from a young age.

You see "WE HAVE VICTORY OVER THE ENEMY" "NOT" JUST SOMETIMES BUT "ALL" OF THE TIME! GOD is our "ROCK" and our "SALVATION" we have nothing to fear. For GOD has not given us a spirit of fear but of "Love and Power" and of a "Sound Mind". God Bless you all and I pray this chapter Bless you as you read it as much as it blessed me to write it. Remember, The Fight Is "FIXED" We Cannot "FAIL" GOD Has Purposed Us to be "WINNERS" Not "LOSERS" "ABOVE" and not "BENEATH" "VICTORIOUS" and not "DEFEATED" As Pastor Joanna Birchett of Harvest House Restoration Center says so boldly, "DEFEAT IS NOT AN OPTION." God Bless you All.

*Words of Reflections*_____

WHEN DOVES CRY

COMPILED BY NEPHETINA L. SERRANO

Special Reflections

WHEN DOVES CRY

My Mother, a Priceless Treasure
By: Terry Moragne-Macon

My mom, Mary Ella Brown Jones Moragne, was short in stature, but a powerful little lady. She stood 4'11 naturally, but was 6' tall in her love and personality. Strength and dignity were her clothing (Prov. 31:25). She was such a presence in our lives, full of wisdom and fun. She was the mother of seven children, six daughters, and one son. She loved the Lord and made sure we knew who He was. She loved her husband and her children. She called him "Hon" and he called her "Sweet."

The loss of my mother was so shattering and

devastating, because it happened so suddenly. That day, mom stopped by my house after work as she usually did, for we lived around the corner from each other. We talked and laughed about a few things, then she said she was going home to let Stephanie, her miniature poodle, out.

Around four hours later, I received a call from my sister, Francine, asking me to go to mom's house to see if she was there. I said, "Yes, she's there because she left my house earlier to let Stephanie out." She said, "Go there anyway." I asked her why, and she responded with a very anxious and on edge voice, "Just do it." I remember this moment so plainly. I said, "I'm not going anywhere until you tell me why." Then she said, "Uncle Felder says mommy is dead." I said, "No way, she was at my house just a few hours ago. Where did they say mom is?" She said, "At the Atlantic City Hospital." Apparently, at the hospital, they looked through mom's personal things, trying to find a family member. It happened to be my uncle who lived in Berlin NJ, and who had mom's same last name. He was at church in Philadelphia and my sister happened to be at the same church that evening. He received the call from one of his daughters informing him of the death of my mother and he in turn informed my sister.

I called Atlantic City Hospital to see if this was true.

Speaking with the nurse who said my mom was there, I asked her, "Is she dead?" She was trying to be professional, but all I wanted to know was if she was really dead. She told me that my mom had passed away from a heart attack. I fell on the floor, acting like a toddler having a fit, screaming and hollering as if I was crazy. After a few moments, the Spirit inside me told me to get up off the floor and see what we needed to do. I got up and got myself together. The nurse was still waiting in the phone, so I asked her, "What do we need to do now?" She said we needed to come and identify the body. All kinds of thoughts went through my mind: How is she going to look? Will I be able to do this? Should I let my children see her? When I tell my other siblings how are they going to act?

I called my siblings and they came immediately. We took five cars and hurried to identify mom's body. She looked so peaceful. Surprisingly, everyone took it well, probably because we were all in shock. Trying to wrap my mind around the fact that mom was talking to me around 6:00pm and around 9:00pm she was dead was extremely difficult. However, I had to transition my mind to do what was necessary, to take care of the business at hand. Even in my grief, I still had to take care of business, making decisions, dealing with finances, with the house, who's going to live there, and so on. I needed to do all of this while feeling numb, and still be the mother and comforter for my three daughters who had just lost a grandmother.

My mom's home-going celebration showed us another aspect of her life. So many people came to her celebration of life service. We sat there asking each other as people passed by, "Do you know her, do you know him?" We didn't know half the people that came to celebrate her life. She made such a positive impact on so many people with her love and generosity, *"For the righteous... will be remembered forever"* (Ps. 112:6).

After everything was over, I had to embrace my grief. This was a process, and everyone's process differs according to the relationship they had with their loved ones. For me, I felt as if a piece of me was severed from my body, as if I went through an amputation surgery.

My mom died on March 7, 1985. I was in grad school getting ready for graduation in May 1985. I lost the desire to go back to school, I was mad with my mom, I was mad with God, I asked Him why He took my mom when there were so many people who didn't love Him, like killers and thieves who were still alive. I felt a little hopeless, performing the daily activities of taking care of my children, but merely existing.

My life, after mom's death, seemed to go in a pace much slower than usual. It was so hard for me to get the energy to carry on. I felt I was in such an unfamiliar place, even though I had lost my father in 1967. My world had been seized by numbness, hurt, pain, anger, and the lack of desire to move on.

One night, I had a dream where my mom came back. It was so real, so plain, and powerful. She came at my front door, wearing the same clothes she had on her last day. She had on her red coat, gray high heels, and her bobbin bag in her hand (she was a seamstress and worked for Botany 500). And this is what she said to me, "Terry, you need to go back to school and finish your degree. You have three children to care for and you must finish what you started." She also said that she tried to tell me she was leaving. I asked her when, she said, "Remember when you said you wanted a bow window for your living room, and I said if I could take that one from my house and give it to you I would?" I said, "How was that telling me you were leaving?" She said, "You know how much I loved my bow window." Then she said, "Remember when we were standing in your dining room and I almost fell over, I was trying to tell you then." She then said, "Go back to school and live your life to the fullest. God has something for you to do." She turned around and went out the door.

I did return to school and received my degree. What was most precious about that was that each one of my sisters wore something of my mother's to my graduation. So, awesome and thoughtful!

The grief process is an on and off situation. Just when you think you are okay, a smell, a song, a picture, or even writing this, wake up emotions, and tears fall. My mom has been dead for over 32 years, and I still sometimes get emotional, especially around Mother's Day. I didn't want to celebrate Mother's Day for years, but it was not fair to my children because I am their mother. When mom first passed away, I would still pick up my phone unconsciously to call her because that was what I did every day. I just wanted to hear her voice.

I hear many people say I don't know what I would do if my mother died. Well, you don't know until it happens to you. In addition, we will all handle it differently and uniquely. What I do know is that God cares for us (1 Pet. 5:7), and He will always be with us through all our hurts.

Healing moves at its own pace, so take it one day at a time. Even though I was angry with God, He was not angry with me. He kept me close to His heart, hid me in the shadow of His wings (Ps. 17:8), and He will do the same for you. He understood my hurt and pain. He, our High Priest, has been tempted as we are (Heb. 4:15), He had to endure His Son's death on the cross. Therefore, He was able to see me as I was, hurt and fragile. He also made me feel His arms wrapped around me with love.

I encourage you who have lost a mother to remember what the Word of God says, Psalm 34:18, *"The Lord is near to the brokenhearted and saves the crushed in spirit;"* Deuteronomy 31:6, *"Be strong and courageous. Do not fear… for it is the Lord your God who goes with you. He will not leave you or forsake you."* He is there with you no matter what, no matter how you feel, no matter what things look like.

The magnitude of pain I felt was a testimony to the love I shared with my mom. And while I don't ever expect to feel alright with the fact that my mom is gone, I know that I am so blessed to have loved my mom and been loved so much by her. I am sure God will do the same for you, for

God shows no partiality (Rom. 2:11). And for those of you who are going through this grief process right now, the pain never goes away altogether, but over time you will find yourself able to go about your life again, just a little different. Be gentle and kind to yourself, and respect each stage of what you're feeling and, as much as you can, be thankful for your mother's love. Keep those precious memories in your thoughts. Remember the things you used to do together, the music you listened to, etc. She would want you to continue living your life like it was GOLDEN.

I declare that every aspect of your life will yield abundant fruit in Jesus' name. I declare that God will enrich your life with an abundance of His joy. I declare that the power, glory, and kingdom of the living God will come upon every aspect of your life, in Jesus' name. I declare you an overcomer in Jesus' name.

Words of Reflections

WHEN DOVES CRY

One of a Kind Mother
By: Carolyn Trumpler-Davis

A real mother knows your every move; she knows when you are happy, she knows when you are sad. She knows when you are well, and she knows when you are sick. A real mother can tell when you have done your best or when you are not really tired. Mothers can see you doing things even when not in their presence. A one of a kind mother is a powerful force, and God has given her talents and skills that many of us will never be able to understand.

When I think of a one of a kind mother, I think of my mother, Lorraine. She was a one of a kind mother. She knew what we needed and she created it, cooked it, made it, or gave her last penny to buy it. She could do things that make us feel we were important and loved. Mom understood our feelings and tried to support us even when she did not agree with our choices.

When I was 5 years old, my mother and my family went to 30th Street station to see a family member who was taking a train home. Somehow, I fell between the platform and the train. I was told afterwards that my mother lied on her stomach with half of her body between the platform and the train trying to get me. The conductor, hearing all the screaming, came to see what was going on, I was running around 6 to 7 feet down between the platform and the train; he lifted me up to my mother. This was the kind of mothers who risk their life for their children.

At age 7 or 8, a pot of hot coffee fell on my back and front leaving me with third degree burns. My mother was giving coffee to my dad and the handle broke off. My mother was there in every step of the way, with all the medical and stabilizing treatments at hospital and home, and this was again a one of a kind mother.

In every situation, school problems, homework, fears, etc. my mother was there for me. As we got older, we became mother and daughter, girlfriends, and buddies who cared for and supported each other in every situation. A one of a kind mother was my mother. She loved people, she loved caring for them, and gave up her own happiness at times to make people happy, and they also loved her. As the years went on and her health began to fail, I started to realize that my great supporter was now the one who needed my support. I tried to be there for her like she was for me.

With everything that is within me I love her and miss her every day, but I remember the life lessons she taught me, and this allows me to go on, and be the women, mother, and friend she taught me to be.

Peace to your soul, Mother Lorraine Dade Trumpler, for all you shared here on this planet. My love forever; you are and you will always be my one of a kind mother.

WHEN DOVES CRY

*Words of Reflections*_____

COMPILED BY NEPHETINA L. SERRANO

WHEN DOVES CRY

COMPILED BY NEPHETINA L. SERRANO

Biographies

WHEN DOVES CRY

VISIONARY
NEPHETINA L. SERRANO

Proverbs 11:14
Where no counsel is, the people fall: but in a multitude of counselors, there is safety.

This evangelist is a, certified life coach, visionary, marriage counselor, inspirational empowerment speaker, advisor mentor and author. She along with her husband is on a quest to rebuild the family one marriage at a time. Evangelist Serrano and husband Richard have one daughter Brande Elise Dora Serrano. They founded Covenant Marriages, Inc. where they are mentoring and coaching couples in crisis who are in need of support during the most challenging times within their marriage. The Serrano's are reaching beyond the walls, helping couples in transitional phases within their marriage and life, restoring the family through biblical counseling. You can hear Evangelist Serrano and her husband every 3rd Thursday on the "We Are One" Empowerment International Conference call and every 2nd and 4th Saturday on The "Healthy Heart" Online Radio Show with Alisha Louis-Potter. She counts it a privilege to serve God's people and a blessing to be called servant.

Evangelist, Nephetina L. Serrano
Co-founder
Covenant Marriages, Inc.
"WE ARE ONE"

Affiliated Businesses, Organizations and Media:
Covenant Rescue 911 – Crisis 24 Hotline
Covenant Marriages Institute
RNS Enterprises, Inc
National Biblical Counseling Association (NBCA)
Email: covenantmarriagesinc@gmail.com
Email: help@covenantrescue911.com
Website: www.covenantmarriagesinc.org
Twitter: CmiMarriages
Facebook: Covenant Marriages, Inc.
Instagram: covenantmarriagesinc
Contact for Bookings Phone (215) 550-1747

FOREWORD

DR. ANNETTE V. HAMPTON

Dr. Annette V. Hampton has been a member of the Christian Stronghold Baptist Church for the past fifty years. She serves as the Counseling Center Director as well as a member of the Exhortation singing ensemble. Dr. Hampton is an instructor for Christian Research and Development where she teaches the advanced biblical counseling training course, abuse and its affects, and the 12 steps with God recovery course designed by Dr. Hampton. This course has inspired many to seek recovery from their addiction patterns. Dr. Hampton has authored a chapter on this topic in *Biblical Perspectives on Tough Issues: Counseling in African American Communities* published by Zondervan.

Dr. Hampton has been a national seminar and workshop speaker for over 35 years. She received her Bachelor's degree from Messiah College, her Master's degree of Science from Shippensburg University, her Master's degree of Social Work from the University of Pennsylvania, and her Ph.D. in Counseling Education and Supervision from Regent University.

Dr. Hampton has been married to Byron L. Hampton for twenty-seven years. They have three children, Benaiah, Anastasia, and Amaris. One of Annette's favorite phrases in Scripture and is Annette's life goal "to serve the Lord her God with all her heart, soul and spirit" with the talents, gifts, and abilities He has blessed her with in this life.

CHAPTER ONE
CARLA GREENE

Evangelist Carla Greene has worked at a young age to support the work of the Lord. As the daughter of Bishop Ernest C Morris and the Late Sylvia Miller Morris, and, by God's divine order, Mother Winifred Morris. She was raised in the church and has initiated, contributed to, and supported many of the 80 auxiliaries that now exist. Her heart ministry was the Drama Ministry, where she produced and wrote plays that were performed in reputable theatres, such as the Meriam Theater in Philadelphia. The Youth Ministry was also in her heart as she served in partnership with her late husband, Elder Walter L. Chavers, for many years.

Evangelist Greene currently supports the Music and Youth Ministry of Mt. Airy COGIC, and serves also in the National Moms of Warriors auxiliary of the Churches of God in Christ. She is also a retired Principal, but continues to work with children at Mt. Airy Christian Day School.

Evangelist Greene is married to Deacon Samuel Greene Jr., another divine order of God. They have three children, Christopher Carl Chavers (30), Stephanie Anne Chavers ESQ (29), and Gabrielle Marie Greene (12).

MOTHER OF CARLA GREENE

CHAPTER TWO
STACI MORGAN BOYD

Staci Morgan Boyd is a member of Beloved Baptist Church, Inc. under the leadership of Rev. Edward and First Lady Donna Duncan Jr. She has been a member since 2008. Staci serves as the Chairlady of the Deaconess Ministry. She is also a member of the choir, and she serves on the Annual Women's Weekend Retreat Committee.

Staci is the Operations Director responsible for improving outcomes for children at the Department of Human Services. She has been married to Deacon Anthony

Boyd for 5 years, and they are the proud parents of Myaah (21), Arren (19) and Lakien (17).

MOTHER OF STACI MORGAN BOYD

CHAPTER THREE
APOSTLE JULIA D. FORD

Apostle Julia Ford is an Assistant Pastor in True Love Church. She is a dedicated vessel of God who thrives in excellence. She is also a devoted wife and a loving mother of three children, Owen III, Julian, and Milan. Moreover, she is a Spiritual Mother to others, and believes in the power of family.

In 2002, Apostle Julia Ford was ordained as the first female Minister at Resurrection Baptist Church in Philadelphia, PA. In 2007, she was ordained as an Elder at Ever Abundant Life Ministries in Darby, PA. Then, in

October 2009, Apostle Julia Ford, along with her husband, Apostle Owen E. Ford, Jr., were "sent out" to begin the work known as "True Love Church" in Folcroft, PA. In March 2011, she was then ordained an Apostle of Jesus Christ. Apostle Julia has now become an author of two books. Her first one is titled *The Fight of My Life*, and her second one *RED* (Resist Every Demon). She also coauthored a book with her husband, *Where He Leads I Will Follow*. She cohosted a radio show called, "Inside the lines." Apostle Julia has also released a song titled "I'll Follow."

Contact Information:

Apostle Julia D. Ford
412 Folcroft Ave
Folcroft, PA 19032
484-493-8748
truelovechurch@hotmail.com

MOTHER OF APOSTLE JULIA FORD

CHAPTER FOUR

RONEVE DAVIS

Roneve Davis is blessed to be part of this project. As a Nursing Home Administrator, and an Executive Director of Assisted Living, Roneve has been in the business of helping families for over 20 years.

Roneve is happily married to Wesley Davis. Their twenty-year union has produced three beautiful children: Justin (25), Tyana (23), and Aleeya (18).

Roneve has a heart for the Lord and will continue to faithfully serve Him and do His will forever. Her prayer is that this book and her personal story will bless people.

MOTHER OF RONEVE DAVIS

CHAPTER FIVE

ANDREA RILEY

Andrea Riley is a licensed Minister, Certified Marriage Specialist, Licensed PAIRS Instructor, and Certified Life Coach. She is cofounder of the "Marriage Service Technicians," an organization dedicated to equipping and empowering relationships, with tools to go the distance. Through this organization, Andrea and her husband, Clifton, teach and mentor couples through workshops, spiritual guidance, speaking engagements, and special events. The couple has been married for 25 years, and they have 4 children and 9 grandchildren.

Andrea also possesses a strong passion for Arts. Her

vision is to create artistic works that have a positive influence upon our culture, leaving an indelible impression on our society, and affecting generations to come. She holds degrees in Entertainment Technology and Business Administration.

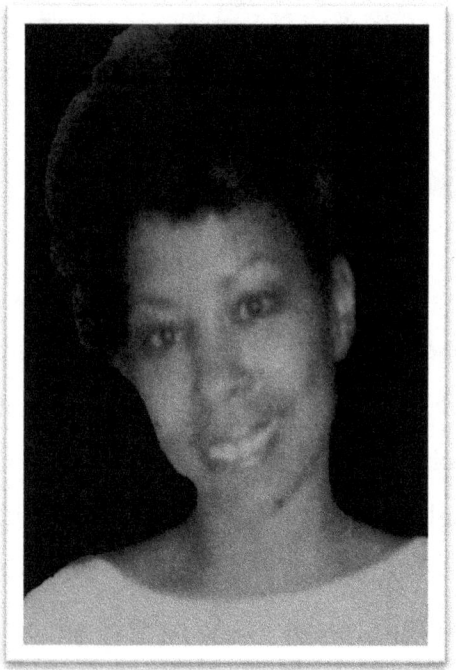

MOTHER OF ANDREA RILEY

CHAPTER SIX

JENNIFER MARLOWE

Evangelist Jennifer Paulette Marlowe is a native of Jamaica, West Indies. During her high school years, dancing was one of her beloved classes. Her exposure to dancing strengthened her interest and passion in it, which ultimately became one of her majors. Her involvement with her high school dance group allowed Jennifer to travel throughout the island of Jamaica performing at various events and participating in numerous competitions. One of her definite wins provided her with a summer program scholarship in Jamaica School of Dance

It was during an evening choir practice when

Jennifer started dancing on the collective voices of the saints that her pastor, Bishop Shawn Bartley, noticed her gift and released her to oversee the praise dance ministry, known as Interpretation of The Word Dance Ministry.

Jennifer is also a fulltime health care worker. She is the proud mother of one child, Odinae Fisher. Evangelist Marlowe's motto is, "Never give away your power."

MOTHER OF JENNIFER MARLOWE

CHAPTER SEVEN

SENATOR LEANNA WASHINGTON

LeAnna Washington started "Women Against Abuse" Organization. Today there is a women's shelter called LeAnna's House, named after then Senator Washington because of her passion for helping women.

In August 2009, she helped organize the first Domestic Violence Walk to raise awareness and funds in order to assist in funding the 24-hours hotline operated by the city of Philadelphia.

In September and December 2013, she authored, and Governor Rendell signed into law, Senate Bill 1147, being the prime sponsor to help local agencies and communities protect children from tragic consequences of neglect and abuse. Senate Bill 1116 was to streamline the investigation of suspected child abuse, and to make sure every incident is investigated in a timely manner.

MOTHER OF LEANNA WASHINGTON

CHAPTER EIGHT

BISHOP MARY FLOYD - PALMER

Bishop Mary Floyd Palmer, affectionately known as Bishop Mary, is the eldest daughter of Rev. Dr. (& the late Mrs. Elizabeth) Melvin Floyd, the legendary and prominent Urban Missionary known as the "Dean of Evangelism."

She is a family woman who resides in Germantown, and is the proud mother of four children and Nana of seven grandchildren. A graduate of the Philadelphia High School For Girls, her educational achievements include a Doctorate of Ministry degree, and the current pursuit of her B.S in Business Administration & Management (Dec. 2018).

Being born into a family where "grass roots evangelism" was the family mantle, Bishop Mary quickly embraced what she knows and loves as Ministry

In 2011, she, along with her ministry partner, Dr. John Thompson Sr., founded The Samaritan Temple, a grass roots church ministry in North Philadelphia, where the focus is not only on salvation of the unsaved through realistic preaching and teaching, but on the desire that all persons will be holistically healed and forever delivered in order to live the abundant life designed by Christ.

CHAPTER NINE

PASTOR JOANNA BIRCHETT

Dr. Joanna Birchett was born in Jamaica, and migrated to the United States at age of 18. She is currently married to her wonderful spouse Apostle Larry Birchett, Jr., who has been a great motivation and inspiration in her life. She is a great mother to her wonderful children, and she is very family oriented. She is the Co-Pastor to her husband, Senior Pastor Apostle Larry Birchett Jr., at The Harvest House Restoration Center in Carlisle, Pennsylvania.

Dr. Birchett is the Founder and CEO of the "Gospel 4 U" Network, and she is well known for her very jovial personality, her love for people, and most of all her prayer life. As the Holy Spirit leads, she operates in the Grace of the Prophetic, a TV host, an author, a journalist, a book publisher, a wife, and mother. She does it all with grace, wisdom, and inspiration of the Holy Spirit. She holds an

Associate Degree in Communication Arts/Journalism, a Bachelor Degree in Public Relations and Marketing, as well as an Honorary Doctoral degree in Humanitarian. She is the author of three books: *Defeat was Never an Option, Stepping Stones* and *The Birthing Process.*

Matthew 11:12 says *"From the days of John the Baptist until now the kingdom of heaven has suffered violence, and the violent take it by force."* This is the principle she lives by.

Contact Information:

For booking and engagements send all inquiries to: info@gospel4unetwork.com, or call: 717-609-0077 or www.gospel4unetwork.com

MOTHER OF DR. JOANNA BIRCHETT

CHAPTER TEN

CORRIE LINGENFELTER

Corrie Lingenfelter is an aspiring author and journalist. She has been writing for over 5 years. Previously, a specialty Restaurant Chef at various resorts, she is now the Public Relations Director at Gospel 4 U Network. She has a degree in Culinary Management from Art Institute of Pittsburgh, and is a recent graduate of Harrisburg Area Community College with an associate degree in Communications/Public Relations. She is currently pursuing a bachelor's degree in Public Relations/Business at Penn State University.

She is the mother of a beautiful 9 years old

daughter, Janessa, and a Deaconess and President of "Singles for Christ" at Harvest House Restoration Center in Carlisle, PA. She is the Founder of "Stay Encouraged," and has dedicated her life to God. She lives to encourage people from all walks of life, and to show the awesomeness of Christ's unfailing love!

MOTHER OF CORRIE LINGENFELTER

CHAPTER ELEVEN

DEIDRA ROUSSAW

Minister Deidra Roussaw married her loving husband, Minister Dwight Roussaw, on August 8, 1998. They exemplify together the portrait of a Christ-centered and Christian-based marriage. They are the proud parents of one daughter, and the loving grandparents of four grandchildren and (a grand angel).

They are licensed and ordained ministers, co-founders of "TWOgether Marriages" and "Kairi's Travel," authors of *Marriage on Fire*, hosts in the Marriage on Fire Radio Show, and also hosts in seminars for spouses by spouses and servant leaders "2 Be One" Marriage Fellowship at The

Resurrection Center under the leadership of Dr. S. Todd & Dr. Cleo V. Townsend, Bishop and Pastor.

Minister Deidra is an author of a book she compiled with over 30 other wives titled *Wives on Fire!* She hosts a monthly wives book club and a monthly "Date Night Tour" alongside her husband. She is currently enrolled in the Success Mastery Coaching Program under the leadership of Dr. Stacia and Arianna Pierce.

MOTHER OF DEIDRA ROUSSAW

CHAPTER TWELVE

ELDER EMMA J. BRANT

Elder Emma J. Brant was born in 1953 to two wonderful parents who parented six beautiful children. She was married in 1985, and she and her husband parented four beautiful children who have all been successful in their own right. Their eldest son is a pastor and their eldest daughter is an evangelist. Their two youngest children are both active in their own successful careers.

In 2001, she joined the Integrity Christian Center Church under the leadership of her son and current Pastor Roosevelt Brant III, Founder and Pastor. Moreover, in 2005, she obtained an Associate of Science Degree (A.A.S.) from the Community College of Philadelphia. Elder Brant went on to study in Alvernia University, where she obtained a Bachelor of Arts Degree (B.A.) in Behavioral Health Studies in 2007, and further obtained a Master of Arts Degree (M.A.) in Community Leadership Counseling in 2010.

Currently, she serves as the Advisor/Chaplain for the Integrity Christian Center (ICCSC), Women's Department, as an Associate Minister, a Mother of the Church, and a member of the Worship Team. In fact, living for the LORD is what she lives for from day to day. She looks forward every day to pleasing GOD and ONLY HIM.

MOTHER OF EMMA JEAN BRANT

SPECIAL REFLECTIONS

TERRY MORAGNE-MACON

Evangelist Terry Moragne-Macon is a native Philadelphian. She went to Community College of Philadelphia, where she received her Associates in Human Services; also to Temple University, where she received her Bachelor and Master's Degrees in Social work. Terry is a member in Mt. Airy COGIC, under the leadership of Pastor/Servant Leader Dr. J. Louis Felton. She serves as an Evangelist in the School of the Prophets, and as an Instructor at Mt. Airy Religious Training Institute (MARTI). Terry is also President and Co-Founder, along with Missionary Lea Sargent, of Divine Intervention International, which is a ministry dedicated to helping children and families especially in Haiti.

She is the wife of Elder Reginald Macon, and the mother of three daughters Lanette, Roben, and DeVonne, and has acquired six more beautiful children; Reginald Jr., Miya, Tamir, Wanda, Robert, and Ferne, as well as twenty-four grandchildren and seven great grandchildren.

MOTHER OF TERRY MORGANE-MACON

Special Reflections

Carolyn E. Trumpler-Davis, AA, BSW, MSW

Carolyn is a practitioner who, through her professional, technical, organizational, and communicational skills, assists clients in resolving and managing circumstances of life. She works currently at Delta Community Support, Inc. for family services as a supervisor for foster care services, and she has been there for over 14 years. She is responsible for the daily management of 110 cases assigned to seven caseworkers.

She has a history of working with professionals such as DHS (The Department of Human Services); the Defenders Association of Philadelphia (Advocates); The Philadelphia Court System; Private Attorneys; ACR

(Achieving Reunification Center for Families in Philadelphia); AI (Achieving Independence Center for Youth in Philadelphia). In addition, Carolyn has experience in working with Microsoft Word, Microsoft Excel, POMP, and evolve System, along with all other devices (copies, fax machines, etc.). Furthermore, for 25 years, Carolyn has served God as a professional Female Gospel Singer throughout the mid-west and eastern US. *The Lord hath done great things for us; whereof we are glad* (Ps. 126:3; KJV).

MOTHER OF CAROLYN E. TRUMPLER-DAVIS

COMPILED BY NEPHETINA L. SERRANO

www.ingramcontent.com/pod-product-compliance
Lightning Source LLC
Chambersburg PA
CBHW070643160426
43194CB00009B/1557